Brothers in Charge

Rochelle Brock and Cynthia Dillard
Executive Editors

Vol. 73

The Black Studies and Critical Thinking series
is part of the Peter Lang Education list.
Every volume is peer reviewed and meets
the highest quality standards for content and production.

PETER LANG
New York • Bern • Berlin
Brussels • Vienna • Oxford • Warsaw

Brothers in Charge

Black Male Leadership in Higher Education and Public Health

Sterling J. Saddler
Maureen P. Bezold
EDITORS

PETER LANG
New York • Bern • Berlin
Brussels • Vienna • Oxford • Warsaw

Library of Congress Cataloging-in-Publication Data

Names: Saddler, Sterling J., editor. | Bezold, Maureen P., editor.
Title: Brothers in charge: black male leadership in higher education and
public health / Sterling J. Saddler, Maureen P. Bezold, editors.
Description: New York: Peter Lang, 2019
Series: Black studies and critical thinking; vol. 73 | ISSN 1947-5985
Includes bibliographical references.
Identifiers: LCCN 2018028587 | ISBN 978-1-4331-3130-1 (hardcover: alk. paper)
ISBN 978-1-4331-3129-5 (pbk.: alk. paper) | ISBN 978-1-4331-5980-0 (ebook pdf)
ISBN 978-1-4331-5981-7 (epub) | ISBN 978-1-4331-5982-4 (mobi)
Subjects: LCSH: African American leadership. | African American college
Administrators—Biography. | African American physicians—Biography.
Classification: LCC E185.615 .B732 2019 | DDC 303.6/408996073—dc23
LC record available at https://lccn.loc.gov/2018028587
DOI 10.3726/b14458

Bibliographic information published by **Die Deutsche Nationalbibliothek**.
Die Deutsche Nationalbibliothek lists this publication in the "Deutsche
Nationalbibliografie"; detailed bibliographic data are available
on the Internet at http://dnb.d-nb.de/.

© 2019 Peter Lang Publishing, Inc., New York
29 Broadway, 18th floor, New York, NY 10006
www.peterlang.com

All rights reserved.
Reprint or reproduction, even partially, in all forms such as microfilm,
xerography, microfiche, microcard, and offset strictly prohibited.

To my mom, Nancy Knight, I offer my thanks and appreciation for the love and support throughout my life as I progressed in my career. Your teaching and values instilled in me the basis to be a sound leader. To my sisters, Shentel and Sonya, who always looked to their big brother for guidance, a constant reminder to do the right thing.

I want to thank my mom, Marion Bezold, who always, always, always believed I could do it even when I didn't believe it. And to my niece Caleigh and my nephews G. T. and Logan for reminding me that the most important leadership role in life is to set a good example for the next generation of leaders. I love you all.

Table of Contents

Acknowledgements	ix
Preface	xi
Chapter One: Effective Leadership	1
Sterling J. Saddler, PhD, Janice L. Glasper, and	
Maureen P. Bezold, PhD, MPH	
Chapter Two: I REMEMBER MAMA SAID ... (The Black Male Leader,	
His Attitudes, Motivation, and Instruction)	33
Alphonso Simpson, Jr, PhD	
Chapter Three: A Call to Lead	45
Georges C. Benjamin, MD, ScD(hc)MACP, FACEP(E), FNAPA,	
Hon FRESPH, Hon FFFP	
Chapter Four: Footsteps of My Father	58
John R. Lumpkin, MD, MPH, FACEP, FACME, FAAN	
Chapter Five: A Darker Shade of Gray: Perpetual Validation of an	
African American University Administrator	76
Sherwood Thompson, EdD	
Chapter Six: Black Male Leadership: Preparing for the Hit in the Gut	94
Keith B. Wilson, PhD, MEd	

Chapter Seven: How Did I Get Here?: Telling My Story 105
    Adewale Troutman, MD, MPH
Chapter Eight: Black Male Leadership 119
    John C. Williams, DrPH, MBA
Chapter Nine: Some Concluding Thoughts 140
    Maureen P. Bezold, PhD, MPH and Sterling Saddler, PhD

About the Editors 143
About the Contributors 145

Acknowledgements

This book would not have come into being without the assistance of a great number of people, and we thank each and every one of you. A number deserve special thanks, among them Georges Benjamin, for his guidance on public health practitioners, and Jerlando Jackson for his conversation about future leaders in higher education. We especially want to extend our gratitude to each of our chapter authors: Georges Benjamin, John Lumpkin, Alphonso Simpson, Sherwood Thompson, Adewale Troutman, John Williams and Keith Wilson. We also thank graduate students Oluwatosin Omoniyi and Ife Oyebode for their diligent work searching for articles relevant to the topics covered in this book. And finally, but by no means last, thank you to Rochelle Brock for having faith in this project, offering valuable suggestions, and exhibiting boundless patience as we worked to complete the manuscript. Again, to each and every one of you, we extend a heartfelt thanks.

Preface

"Whatever we believe about ourselves and our ability comes true for us."
—Susan L. Taylor

Picking cotton. Surviving New York winters without heat. Living in the projects. Is this the stuff of leaders? You will learn that it is. You will read the stories of seven African American men who have risen to leadership positions in their fields, most of whom come from humble beginnings. But first we want to introduce you to what leadership really is. It will become apparent to you that no single definition, list of descriptors, or specific style of leadership works for every organization and that the future of effective leadership will mean having an understanding of yourself as leader, your followers, and your organization's vision for future endeavors. We have identified some sobering statistics pertaining to leadership.

The U.S. Bureau of Labor Statistics (2012) reported that in 2011, black males held 9.7% of management positions in the U.S., and its data indicates black males are more likely to be represented in education. Jackson (2006) states:

> national-level data demonstrated that, although white males continue to hold the overwhelming majority of academic leadership positions, African American males have made modest advancements in upper level administrative positions at specific types of higher and post-secondary educations institutions (e.g., 2-year and private institutions). More specifically, these results suggested that a disparate impact exists

between the hiring of African American males and white males in academic leadership positions. (p. 316)

It is difficult to enumerate the public health workforce because the field is exceptionally broad. However, in 2012, local governmental public health officials reported that 40% of the leaders are men, a drop of 4% since 2005 (National Association of County and City Health Officials [NACCHO], 2013). In addition, only 7% of these leaders were not white, a drop of 1% since 2005 (NACCHO, 2013).

While these numbers are low, this volume shares the stories of seven African American men who have attained leadership positions in both higher education and public health. We hope this volume inspires other people to seek leadership positions in these disciplines. We chose these disciplines because of the intimate relationship between education and health status. Research suggests that the greater one's educational attainment, the better one's health. Because of the significant chronic diseases found in the black community particularly among males, there needs to be more high-profile black male leaders and administrators in institutions that serve all Americans.

CHAPTER ONE

Effective Leadership

STERLING J. SADDLER, PhD, JANICE L. GLASPER,
AND MAUREEN P. BEZOLD, PhD, MPH

"Never underestimate the power of dreams and the influence of the human spirit. We are all the same in this notion: The potential for greatness lives within each of us."
—WILMA RUDOLPH

Effective Leadership: Principles, Practices, and Styles in the Workforce Leadership Yesterday

The history of leadership begins with the Trait Theory of Leadership in which early descriptors of leadership assigned particular traits to those who became leaders (Daresh, 2001, p. 108). The traits of effective leaders were classified as those relating to personality, physical appearance, social background, intelligence and ability. People believed their presence separated leaders from followers, and even, effective leaders from ineffective leaders (Dessler, 1980, p. 206). Most of the early research related to trait theories was found to be inconclusive; that is, many of the traits were considered crucial to leadership in one study were not found to be crucial in another, as summarized by Taylor (1994). Although the search for specific traits in effective leaders has not produced a list that can be used exclusively, it is apparent from the literature that lists of attributes of "successful" or "effective" leaders continue to be generated. Other traits of effective leadership identified by researchers include interpersonal skills and the ability to inspire and motivate subordinates to carry out the vision necessary for organizational survival (Trott & Windsor, 1999).

According to Clark (1997) a leader needs to interact with followers, peers, seniors, and other people whose support is needed by an organization to accomplish its objectives. An effective leader must be able to understand and motivate the people around him. To do this, the leader must have an understanding of human nature that is the common quality of all human beings and crucial to becoming an effective leader. In his leadership research on human nature, Clark takes an in-depth look at the theories of experts in the field of human nature. These theories and experts include: Abraham Maslow's—Theory of Hierarchical Needs; Frederick Herzberg's—Hygiene and Motivational Factors; and Douglas McGregor's—Theory X and Theory Y, to name a few. By understanding some of these theories of human nature, and how they help motivate followers, Clark proposes that one can become an effective leader.

Another theory of leadership, the Situational Theory, maintains that leadership is determined less by the characteristics of the individual than by the requirements of the group or setting in which the individual works (Daresh, 2001, p. 109). The Situational Theory of Leadership proposes that leadership is brought about more by the goals and demands of the group and that these acts of leadership are a direct result of group interactions. Taylor (1994) summarized the concept of situational leadership by saying: "It is useful to think of leadership as a generic term which refers to the processes characterized by the interrelationships among people as they work together in the formulation and achievement of shared goals".

The final theory to be discussed from the early years of leadership development is the Behavioral Theory of Leadership, which tends to focus more on how leaders behave, rather than their leadership traits or their interactions with groups. Daresh (2001) proposes that a leader's behavior is the result of a combination of both personal characteristics as well as the situations in which the leader must act.

The basic assumptions of this view of leadership are;

- people behave according to different leadership styles because people differ in how they perceive a situation, accomplish tasks, interact with others, and make decisions,
- people behave differently, depending on contextual circumstances,
- there is no single "right way" for people to behave,
- what is comfortable and "right" for one person may feel uncomfortable and "wrong" to another,

- an organization functions best when it capitalizes on the strengths of each individual, encouraging the recognition and celebration of differences. (Daresh, 2001, p. 110)

Research based on these assumptions of behavioral leadership led to the development of models that have been used to illustrate and/or diagnose particular leadership styles or particular aspects of leader behavior (Taylor, 1994). Furthermore, if any single approach to the study of leadership can be classified as the prevailing perspective of the last quarter-century or more, it would be the behavioral approach (Daresh, 2001, p. 110), for it was the behavioral theories of leadership, that first started researchers to revise and develop different leadership styles, some of which have become prevalent in the workforce of today.

Leadership Today

The desires to understand, define, and explain the essence of leadership has interested researchers and scholars for most of the twentieth century. In their efforts to find an "accurate and precise" definition of leadership, thousands of studies have been published in the last several decades. Most of these explanations have focused on a single person and his or her personal qualities and skills. Scientists have tried to identify what abilities, traits, behaviors, sources of power or aspects of the situation determine how effectively a leader will be able to influence others (Brungardt, 1998).

But, before we go any further into leadership; before we attempt to define leadership; before we try to determine exactly what leaders do and what it means to lead; let us try to determine exactly what *leadership is not*.

During the last fifty years there has been an explosion of books and consultants focused on promoting management and leadership. Yet the fact remains that much confusion exist today, even about the very definition of the word *leadership!* In our society today we have difficulties differentiating between those individuals who beneficially change our time and organizations by attaining remarkable achievements, from the highly ambitious who simply claw their way to the top with no regard for anyone else involved. Modem culture has a tendency to refer to people in both categories as "leaders". For instance, you will hear how a business executive or CEO has been convicted of a crime, and yet will still be regarded as a "business leader"! Society tends to identify these people as leaders just because they have gained control of an organization, regardless of how they arrived at that position or how ineptly they have ruled.

In our western culture we continue to degrade the real position and achievement of such individuals as Thomas Jefferson, Abraham Lincoln, Winston Churchill, and Martin Luther King Jr. who guided others in attaining incredible progress—by placing people like Adolph Hitler, Joseph Stalin, and Saddam Hussein—whose lives were dedicated to manipulation and control over others no matter what the cost—in the same classification. Yes! We group the manipulators in with the visionaries and call them both leaders. Unfortunately, we as a society have not reached a point where we can articulate the difference. This is unfortunate because when we think about the accomplishments of both groups ... there is a very clear distinction (weLead, 2001).

> A real modern leader is a servant first! Secondly, the servant-leader aspires to lead in order to produce positive change. The leader's main goal is to help the followers grow as individuals. This allows them freedom to reach their needs as they become more autonomous, wiser, and productive. In turn, they also become servant leaders once will model those who have earned their credibility and respect. (Thomas, 2001a, p. 2)

> The chief executive who knows his strengths and weaknesses as a leader is likely to be far more effective than the one who remains blind to them. He also is on the road to humility, that priceless attitude of openness to life that can help a manager absorb mistakes, failures, or personal shortcomings. (McCarty, 2001, p. 3)

So what does it mean to be a leader? Let us move on to defining what it means to lead, and take an in-depth look at some of the qualities of successful leaders and effective leadership.

The Webster's II New College Dictionary (1995) defines the term *lead* as "meaning to show the way by going in advance". It defines the term *leader* as "one that leads or guides, or the one in charge or in command of others". It defines *leadership* as "the position or office of a leader; or the capacity or ability to lead". Contrary to popular opinion, the term "leadership" is a relatively new term to the English language. It did not come into usage until the late nineteenth century (Brungardt, 1998). These definitions are vague and leave too much to the imagination. They don't give you a specific enough interpretation of what it means to lead. There is much more to leadership than is stated in the dictionary. We have come across numerous definitions of leadership provided by various experts in the field of leadership studies. But the best one was provided Thomas (2001) who said:

> Leadership is the ability to articulate a vision, to embrace the values of that vision, and nurture a positive environment where everyone can reach the organization's goals and their own personal needs. This means that leaders effectively combine individuals

and resources together to accomplish things that would be virtually impossible to achieve alone! It does not require power, prominence, charisma or dozens of followers to be a leader. Leadership is a value-based philosophy, not a collection of tricks, tips, gestures and the right words during a time of need. Leadership authority James O'Toole reminds us that a leader's vision becomes the follower's vision "because it is built on a foundation of their needs and aspirations. They see in the vision what they desire, and they embrace it as their own." O'Toole continues that, "There are no contingencies here; the only course for the leader is to build a vision that followers are able to adopt as their own *because it is their own*." (p. 1)

Another excellent definition of leadership, written by Clark (1997) states that:

> Leadership is a complex process by which a person influences others to accomplish a mission, task, or objective and directs the organization in a way that makes it more cohesive and coherent. A person carries out this process by applying his/her leadership attributes (belief, values, ethics, character, knowledge, and skills). (p. 1)

> Good leaders are made not born (Clark, 1997). They are developed through a never-ending process of self-study, education, training, and experience. The only requirement is that one has the willpower and the desire to become a good leader, as it requires continued hard work and studying to improve leadership skills.

How to Become a Successful Leader

Bernard Bass' (1989) theory of leadership, states that there are three basic ways to explain how people become leaders. The first two, which include the Trait Theory and the Great Events Theory, explain the leadership development for a small number of people. The Trait Theory implies that some personality traits may lead people naturally into leadership roles. The Great Events Theory implies that situations of crisis or important events may cause a person to rise to the occasion, which brings out extraordinary leadership qualities in an ordinary person. The third way involves choosing to become a leader and learning leadership skills. This is the Transformational Leadership Theory which will be discussed later. Bass (1989) believed that when a person is deciding if he/she respects you as a leader, he/she does not think about your traits or qualities. Instead, they observe what you do so they know who you really are. Are you honorable and trustworthy, or are you a self-serving person who misuses authority to look good and get promoted? Self-serving leaders are not very effective because their employees only obey them, they do not respect or follow them (Clark, 1997). Furthermore, the basis of good leadership is honorable character and selfless service to the organization. In your employees' eyes, your leadership is everything that you do that affects the organization's objectives and their well-being. This is important to remember because people want to be guided by those they respect and those who have a clear sense of direction.

Many factors influence the success of an organization's leader. Some important key factors of successful leadership are listed below.

- Leaders must model management behavior to fit their immediate subordinates. In other words, the leader must behave in the same way he wants those he manages or supervises to behave. No double standards.
- Successful leaders clearly communicate specific performance expectations to their followers. Subordinates should be given the freedom to make decisions and give input, but the limits of that freedom should be well defined.
- The best leaders don't tolerate incompetence anywhere in their organizations. They hold people accountable for the expected performance.
- Successful leaders see that procedures are in place so that direction of the workforce is not left to chance, thereby influencing how all people in the organization behave and perform.
- Successful leaders are not lazy—they work hard and are usually very self-confident which can improve the probability of organizational success.
- Successful leaders know when to make decisions and usually have a strong concern for completing objectives and solving problems. They avoid excessive consensus and compromise. Poor leaders tend to avoid decisions if the consequences might upset someone: they defer the responsibility for tough decisions to others.
- Leaders must have effective interpersonal skills for coaching subordinates and for gently and relentlessly enforcing the organization's standards of performance.
- Equity is crucial for trust and morale in an organization. Effective leaders don't play favorites. They practice a high degree of objectivity and fairness in all their actions.
- The best leaders have control over the communication process between themselves, at the top, and those at the bottom of the organization. Effective leaders place a very high priority on open, timely and valid communication and make it happen throughout the organization. (Clark, 2000; Kent, 2004; Rubenstein, 2004; weLead Magazine, 2001)

The successful leader possesses strong beliefs, values and positive attitudes and is responsible for creating a culture, determining values and passing on principles that will give a direction to the organization or business. Being a successful leader is no longer a position of status. It's about having the power to inspire and motivate subordinates to achieve goals. The ability to motivate followers is the force that will take the goals of the organization to the limits (Magalhaes, 2001). This is accomplished by the facilitation of groups of people in adopting a common vision and creates effective results (Magalhaes, 2001).

James McGregor Burns, a well-known researcher in the field of leadership, wrote a significant book in the 1970s entitled *Leadership*. In his book he attempts to define the processes or behaviors used by leaders to motivate or influence followers. Burns (1978) described leadership behavior as falling within two broad categories of influence. One category is called *transactional* leadership and the other category is called *transformational* leadership (Thomas, 2003).

Transactional Leadership—A form of leadership whereby followers are motivated based on their own self-interest. In other words, transactional behavior focuses on the accomplishment of tasks and good worker relationships in exchange for desirable rewards (Thomas, 2003). Followers are motivated by the leader's promises, praise, and reward, or, they are corrected by negative feedback, reproof, threats, or disciplinary actions (Bass & Steidlmeier, 1998). Furthermore, subordinates understand their job roles and the expectations set for them by the leader and organization. In addition, employees are motivated and directed to achieve "expected" standards of performance because transactional leaders clarify what followers receive for the specific level of effort and/or performance required of them (Avolio, Waldman, & Yammarino, 1991).

Transactional leadership can encompass four types of behavior.

1. *Contingent Reward*—To influence behavior, the leader clarifies the work or goals to be accomplished and uses rewards, praise, promises or incentives to motivate followers to accomplish those goals.
2. *Passive Management by Exception*—To influence behavior, the leader uses correction, reprimands, negative feedback, reproof, threats, or disciplinary actions as a response to unacceptable performance by subordinates. But the passive manager/leader, waits until mistakes are brought to his/her attention before taking corrective action
3. *Active Management by Exception*—To influence behavior, the leader actively monitors the work performed and uses corrective methods to ensure the work is completed to meet accepted standards.
4. *Laissez-Faire Leadership*—The leader is indifferent and has a "hands-off" approach toward workers and their performance. The leader ignores the needs of others, does not respond to problems or does not monitor performance. In other words, the leader using this style of motivation avoids leading. (Bass & Steidlmeier, 1998; NetGuide, 2000; Thomas, 2003)

Transactional leadership behavior is the traditional form of leadership used to one degree or another by most leaders. However, a leader should not exclusively or primarily practice transactional leadership to influence others, because leadership effectiveness is based on an understanding of the tasks at hand, the leader and his/her skills, the followers and their skills and the situation. The leader must take all of these parts into consideration before deciding on how followers should be motivated.

Transformational Leadership—"A form of leadership that occurs when leaders broaden and elevate the interests of their employees, when they generate awareness and acceptance of the purposes and the mission of the group and when they stir their employees to look beyond their own self-interest for the good of the group" (Bass, 1990).

The heart of transformational leadership is the leader's desire and ability to raise the consciousness of others by appealing to powerful moral values and ideals (Thomas, 2003). These leaders trust their subordinates and leave them space to breathe and grow (Epitropaki, 2001). The transformational leader is able to transform followers beyond the dishonorable emotions of jealousy, greed, and fear to higher principles of liberty, justice and humanitarianism. Transformational leaders serve as teacher, mentor, and coach to their superiors, peers, and subordinates in an attempt to elevate and empower them to a higher level of commitment and growth (Thomas, 2003). They themselves take personal risks and are not afraid to use unconventional but always ethical methods to achieve the desired goal (Epitropaki, 2001). Transformational leaders can be found within any organization and at any level in the organization. They have a clear collective vision of where their group, department, or organization should be heading. And, most importantly, they manage to communicate that vision effectively to all employees.

Today it is acknowledged that there are four distinct characteristics exhibited by transformational leaders. These characteristics are collectively called the "Four I's of Transformational Leadership" (Avolio et al., 1991).

1. *Individualized Consideration*—Transformational leaders pay attention to the individual employee and his/her needs rather than labeling all followers alike and having the same needs. They listen and share an individual's concerns while simultaneously helping to build the individual's confidence. The transformational leader often "goes to bat" for the employee whenever necessary, making sure that the employee has the help and resources necessary to achieve the current goals (Avolio et al., 1991). Transformational leaders attempt to remove unnecessary obstacles in the system that could inhibit both the development of followers and their achieving optimum performance. This behavior provides coaching, support and encouragement of specific followers as indicated by their needs (Thomas, 2003). The transformational leader must be able to diagnose and evaluate the needs of

each follower, understand that those individualized needs will change over time partially based on the influence of the leader (Avolio et al., 1991).
2. *Intellectual Stimulation*—Through intellectual stimulation, transformational leaders help followers think about nagging problems in new and unique ways. As a result of this intellectual stimulation by their leaders, followers develop their own capabilities to recognize, understand, and eventually solve future problems (Avolio et al., 1991). An intellectually stimulating leader arouses in followers an awareness of problems, a sensitivity to each ones thoughts and imagination, and a recognition of the beliefs and values of the leader and his/her followers (Thomas, 2003).
3. *Inspirational Motivation*—This behavior exhibited by transformational leaders, models high values and includes communication of an inspiring vision that is shared by workers/followers (Thomas, 2003). The inspirational leader often sets an example of hard work, gives "pep" talks, remain optimistic in times of crisis, and searches to reduce an employees' duties and workloads by using creative work methods (Avolio et al., 1991).
4. *Idealized Influence*—This behavior exhibited by leaders arouses followers to feel a powerful identification and strong emotions toward the leader. The transformational leader accomplishes this by showing respect for others and by building their confidence and trust in the overall mission. When followers observe their leaders achieving desired results, the followers are more likely to want to emulate the leader in terms of the leaders behaviors, attitudes and values. In other words, the truly transformational leader can show his or her followers that they can accomplish objectives that they felt were impossible, thereby achieving their full potential and providing benefits to all concerned. (Avolio et al., 1991; NetGuide, 2000)

The end result of transformational leadership is empowering others to take more initiative in their work, inspiring them to be more commanding and building their self-confidence. Transformational leaders accomplish these goals by nurturing an organizational culture, giving attention to priorities and concerns, maturely reacting to crisis situations, role modeling, engaging in wise allocation of rewards, and by defining the criteria for success (Thomas, 2003).

Effective leaders of today's workforce must use the principles of both leadership styles when attempting to motivate followers.

Successful Leadership and Human Relations

1. The six most important words: "I admit I made a mistake."
2. The five most important words: "You did a good job."

3. The four most important words: "What is your opinion?"
4. The three most important words: "If you please."
5. The two most important words: "Thank you."
6. The one most important word: "We."
7. The least important word: "I." (Clark, 1997)

Just consider how much better the workforce could be if these seven principles of successful leadership were followed in every organization. For this to happen, you must learn to develop the invisible world of people's minds and to open the human heart, for it is by the actions of followers that leaders are born (Magalhaes, 2001). Followers have a choice to support who or what they desire and if they are not satisfied, they will vote with their feet … they walk away. No longer will followers accept situations where the leaders get what they want at the expense of the followers. Don't misunderstand, people are still willing to be followers, especially for a good or noble cause, but they expect more from their leadership. They expect their leaders to care about them, to treat them with dignity and respect, to act responsibly and help them to meet their needs. Any leader who fails to do this will soon lose his followers either physically, emotionally and/or spiritually (Thomas, 2001).

Understanding the Leader/Follower Relationship

There are four main concepts involved in the relationships between leaders and followers that must be understood to be successful. They include the follower, the leader, communication/commitment, and the situation.

Follower Different people require different styles of leadership. You must know your people! The basic starting point for this is to have a good understanding of human nature as well as the needs, emotions, and motivational requirements of your subordinates. Consequently, no one style of leadership will work for every follower. Therefore, your style as a leader must vary depending on the particular follower or group of followers (Clark, 2000). Not everyone becomes a leader, but those who follow are no longer accepting old-fashioned leaders with authoritative ideas and no regard for those he leads. They want leaders with well-rooted human values, who show respect for the talent and contributions made by others. People want leaders who can create an environment of risk and creativity. They reject intimidation or manipulation and want to be recognized as an important part of the workforce in the organization or industry (Magalhaes, 2001).

Leader You must have an understanding of who you are, what you know, and what you can do. Remember it is the followers who determine if a leader is successful, not the leader. Followers who lack trust or confidence in their leader will be uninspired. You as the leader must convince your followers that you are worthy of being followed (Clark, 2000). But first, leaders must look within themselves to find new ways of influencing people and changing the course of organizations. It is the leader who must be the first to change. The leader can then gather mature and responsible people who are personally committed to themselves and the success of the organization. The leader has the obligation to take command, establish rules, determine values, and set forth principles that will lead to success of the organization as a whole. At the same time, he must look at leadership as a responsibility, not as a position of privileges. The effective leader is responsible for all final decisions and he must not fear the force of his associates or subordinates. The effective leader is proud of all those that collaborate with him and he looks at the success of others as being his as well (Magalhaes, 2001). Effective leaders in the workforce always have advisors, partners and supporters by their sides and have become successful because they enabled *others* to achieve greatness and allowed themselves to *follow* (Zust, 2001b). Effective leaders know how and when to follow. By following, they know when to shut up and listen, set aside their ego for the greater good, and take pride in sharing a collective vision so that everyone can benefit. Ineffective leaders fail to understand the concept of being a follower. They don't listen to advice when it's given, and they certainly don't ask for advice when they need to, because they feel this will be perceived as weakness. In reality, the best leaders welcome advice and admit they don't have all the answers (Zust, 2001b).

Communication/Commitment—You can become a successful leader through two-way communication, much of which is non-verbal. You set the example by your actions, without having to say a word. This could either build or harm the relationship between you and your employees depending on what your non-verbal communications portray to your employees. Believing in the vision of the organization, no matter how passionately is not enough. A leader must be able to communicate the vision frequently, effectively, and in different ways to different constituents. Great communication is the ability to take something complicated and making it simple (Wolfson, 2002). Commitment through words alone is not enough. People in any organization are "professional boss watchers", and will ultimately mimic the behaviors of the leaders of organization. So ... an effective leader is very careful about his verbal communications, but he is even more careful about in physical actions, because in the realm of leadership, actions speak much louder than words (Wolfson, 2002). As the followers observe you as the leader, they will be acutely aware of how you make and honor your commitments, what you say in formal and especially informal settings, what yours interests are and the questions you ask, where you go and who you spend your time with; How and when you act/ who you consult with and how you organize your staff and your physical surroundings. Yes ... your followers will watch your every move before they determine if you are a leader worth following. Remember, communication, whether verbal or non-verbal, is not always easy, and can be especially taxing when taking into consideration that the workforce is filled with a diverse population. This population is composed of individuals with different cultures and ethnicities, with different religious and sexual orientations, as well as individuals from different generations, each with his own set of values, beliefs and attitudes. Of all the issues involved with communication as a leader, communication across generations can be the most difficult to perform. Zust (2001a) states that: "We (the Baby Boomer Generation), are the 'sandwich leaders,' the first generation squeezed between managing and leading people older than us (Traditionalists) and those following in our footsteps (Generations X and Y)" (p. 4). While her paper is entitled "Baby Boomer Leaders Face Challenges Communicating Across Generations," (2001a), she gives some very sound advice on how leaders of any generation can communicate across the generation gap and diversity of today's workforce.

Situation—All situations, like all people, are different and what you do in one leadership situation may not always work in another situation. Use your judgment to decide the best course of action and the leadership style needed for each situation (Clark, 2000).

There are a number of forces that will affect these factors such as your relationships with your seniors, the skill of your employees, the informal leaders within your organization and the organizational structure of the company itself, but the successful leader must know how to deal with these situations in the most effective and efficient manner, always taking into consideration everyone involved as well as the organization as a whole.

Leadership, Organizational Culture, and Climate

There are two distinct forces that determine how to act within an organization: They are organizational **culture and climate.**

Every organization has its own distinctive culture that is a combination of the founders, past and current leadership, crises, events, history, and size. *All* of which represent the organization's routines, rituals, and the "way we do things." This organizational culture determines what it takes to be in good standing and directs the accepted behavior for each circumstance (Clark, 2000). It deals with assumptions that have been made about both the internal and external worlds, an organization faces. Once these assumptions become grounded and widely shared by the organizational members, they become the basis of that organization's culture (Munro & Beeson, 2002). Once the culture of an organization exists, it determines the criteria for leadership. This culture determines who will or will not become an organization's leader. As a result, the leaders who emerge are themselves a reflection of the organization's values. Simply stated, leadership and culture are intertwined. It is the responsibility of leadership to perceive both the functional and dysfunctional elements of the existing culture. If the organization's leaders are not aware of the culture of their work environment, the culture will manage them. Therefore, leadership's task is to manage cultural evolution and change in such a way that the organization can survive in a changing environment (Munro & Beeson, 2002). But, for this to occur, the organization as a whole must attain a culture of understanding between all of its members. In addition, the organization's leadership and staff must have the commitment, dedication and time required to initiate the creation of a *culture of understanding* (Munro & Beeson, 2002).

The following five basic steps can provide the foundation for development of a culture of understanding within an organization.

1. Commitment to a process of intent and inquiry.
2. Review of organizational purpose (mission statement/vision).
3. Initiation of the process of leadership dialogue.
4. Encouragement of inquiry at all levels of the organization.
5. Development of open feedback channels-both internally and externally. (Munro & Beeson, 2002)

Creating this environment of a *culture of understanding* will provide organizations with the necessary creativity and flexibility to deal with increasing complexities and challenges of today's global environment.

The organizational climate represents the "feel" of the organization, the individual and shared perceptions and attitudes of its members. This perception of the organization comes from what the people believe about the activities that occur in the organization. Such activities include the items listed below.

- How well does the leader clarify the priorities and goals of the organization?
- What is the system of recognition, rewards, and punishments in the organization?
- How competent are the leaders?
- Are leaders free to make decision?
- What will happen if I make a mistake?

Organizational climate is based on the values, attributes, skills, and actions, as well as the priorities of the leader. In other words, organizational climate is directly linked to the leadership and management style of the leader.

Things are done differently in every organization. The collective vision and common folklore that define the institution are a reflection of culture. Individual leaders cannot easily create or change culture. Culture influences the characteristics of the climate by its effect on the actions and thought processes of the leader. But, everything one does, as a leader will affect the climate of the organization (Clark, 2000). Effective leaders will have done their homework to discover what the organizational culture and climate are, long before he/she becomes a part of that organization.

Leadership, Trust, and Diversity

One of the great challenges facing any organization is getting all of its employees, from the top leaders to the hourly workers, to realize that to become the best, they have to embrace diversity (Clark, 2001). Embracing diversity remains one of the most challenging obstacles facing leaders of any organization. Individual biases and prejudices are found deeply rooted with in every individual and they shape our perceptions about how we do things and how we respond in certain situations (Clark, 1994). Even as international trade and technological innovation are helping to create a global society, the world seems at the same time to be more fragmented and divided.

How can we develop genuine and sustained mechanisms to foster greater understanding and social cohesion for people with diverse values, perspectives, needs, and strengths (W.K. Kellogg Foundation, 2003)? As a leader in an organization, it is your responsibility to create a culture of shared values, vision and trust where your subordinates know what to expect and participate because it is what they want to do. Leadership cannot take place in a culture where people distrust each other, doubt other's motives, and pursue their own ideas and agendas (Reese, 2003). Trust is central to leadership because it is the trust of followers that allows leaders to lead. There can be no leaders without followers, but ... to follow, people must believe in the same core organizational values as their leaders. Successful leaders create this culture of values and live and work by them, thereby, building the trust of their followers by the actions they take and the words they speak. Fairholm (1994) defines trust as reliance on the integrity, or authenticity, of other people. He believed that developing a trust culture is critical to leadership success and that a leader has the prime responsibility to create culture in which trustworthiness is an integral part of the organization's culture. This culture affects willingness to trust, and willingness to trust is directly related, but not limited to, diversity issues in the workforce. For example, for a leader to obtain a competitive edge he must create great work teams by using the full potential of every individual. In these teams, each individual must understand each other, support each other, and trust each other to accomplish its mission. Personal agendas, biases, and prejudices should not be tolerated by any team member because if the members don't accept each other for whom and what they are, they will not be able to use the abilities of all the members to fill in the weak spots. The effective leader understands that embracing diversity is the first item for building teams and to build a great team, there must be a diverse group of people on the team. Effective leaders avoid choosing people who are alike or share similar views. Instead, he chooses people from a variety of backgrounds and cultures. The one thing the team members must have in common is organizational culture. But before the leader can obtain a sense of organizational culture from his followers perspective, he must first gain an appreciation for the diversity of his employees.

Although diversity includes race, religions, gender, sexual orientation including LGBTQ, national origin, ethnicity and so on, it goes beyond that to include individual biases and prejudices, all of which must be dealt with effectively to ensure the success of the organization (Clark, 2001). If the leaders of the organization don't address the challenges of diversity, it soon becomes extinct or at the very least is left far behind. Organizations have to realize that the world is culturally diverse and represents potential customers. To attract a wide variety of customers, organizations must become multicultural themselves. People of other cultures will no longer tolerate organizations that don't employ "people of their kind", especially in leadership, and high-visibility positions. Instead, people will spend their money with organizations that truly believe in diversity. So … it is the organization's leaders who are responsible for articulating policies that govern diversity. But embracing diversity is more than tolerating people who are different. It means actively welcoming and involving them by engaging in the practices listed here.

- Developing an atmosphere that is safe for all employees to ask for help. Building great teams by joining together the strengths and weaknesses of each member to get the goal accomplished.
- Actively seeking information from people from a variety of backgrounds and cultures.
- Including people who are different than you in informal gatherings such as lunch, coffee breaks, and spur of the moment meetings.
- Creating a team spirit in which every member feels like they belong.

In addition, successful leaders become visibly involved in programs that affect organizational changes in culture because doing so displays leadership that eradicates oppression of all forms, at all levels of the organizations structure, and illustrates commitment to diversity.

Leadership and Ethics

No discussion of leadership would be complete without an examination of another very important element—ethics. At the moment, America is experiencing a crisis of confidence in its leaders, mostly due to constant coverage by newspapers, press conferences, radio, and television broadcasts of leaders caught in unethical situations. It seems we hear or read more stories about unethical practices in our leadership representatives, than not.

Leaders should be held accountable for their actions and are expected by their followers to demonstrate ethical behavior at all times. This expectation of ethical behavior is not a new concept, but the recent intense coverage of unethical practices in leadership by the media may be. This intense coverage has resulted in increased calls by the public for accountability and regulation.

To become an effective leader, you should follow a constant path of self-evaluation and practice several standards of ethical excellence. These standards, according to Haughey (1995), should include: Ethical communication; ethical quality; ethical collaboration; ethical succession planning, and ethical tenure.

> *Ethical Communication*—Ethical leaders set the standard of truth for every employee they lead. The moment people take on the position of a leader they have an opportunity to place the highest premium on truthfulness and every form of communication put forth by a leader should be an accurate representation.
>
> *Ethical Quality*—Leaders must champion the process of quality throughout the organization in order to ensure the global competitiveness of the organization. It is the leader's responsibility to drive, steer, and fund the quality initiative throughout the organization. For only when top leaders fully endorse a quality initiative does it have a chance of becoming fully implemented and then reap the harvest by having a quality product, quality customer service, and quality delivery of that product.
>
> *Ethical Collaboration*—Effective leaders pick the most astute individuals as advisors. They surround themselves with answers. Through this collaboration with trustworthy individuals, leaders gain advice on incorporating best practices, solving problems, and addressing the issues facing their organization.
>
> *Ethical Succession Planning*—Ethical leaders set aside issues of "turf" and let other leader's surface within the organization, giving potential successors opportunities to exercise and build their leadership skills. This is performed to ensure the long-term success of the organization once the current leaders have moved on. Once the potential successors have been identified, they should be mentored by the leader, given opportunities to prove themselves and trained for the roles they may one day assume.
>
> *Ethical Tenure*—How long should a leader lead? There are no formal standards governing the length of tenure. But, ethical leaders feel they lead at the

request of the company, customers, board of directors, and stockholders. As long as the entity's trust in the leader remains unchallenged, the leader should lead until he or she chooses to step down. However, effective leaders also know that eventually they must give the reins of the organization to a new set of watchful eyes.

Facing Ethical Dilemmas—When faced with an apparent ethical dilemma, leaders who want to be successful should ask themselves the following questions.

1. Is it legal? That is, does it break any laws?
2. Is it balanced? Is it fair to all concerned, or does it give one party or group extreme advantage over another party? Does it promote win-win relationships?
3. How will it make me feel about myself? Would I want my family to know about this? How would I feel if this were published on the front page of my hometown newspaper? (Blanchard & Peale, 1988, p. 20)

According to Blanchard and Peale (1988), honest evaluation and application of this checklist should result in ethical leadership.

Ethical leadership is one of the most important qualities of successful leadership. It is the glue that holds the organization and its members together. Simplistically put, ethics is learning the difference between right and wrong and then doing the right thing (Price, 2001). But often doing the right thing is not as simple and straightforward as it may sound. Also, standards of right and wrong are often based on the individual's personal values. Within a work environment, the cultural values that drive business decisions are critical to the organization's credibility, it's employees, customers, and shareholders. Given the recent examples of breech of professional ethics—such as the Bernie Madoff fiasco—organizations of all kinds are being forced to take a hard look at their own mode of operating to determine just how credible their organization appears to both their employees and their public. Remember perception is reality (Price, 2001).

Philosophers have been discussing ethics since the time of Socrates and Plato, at least 2500 years. Today an organization's ethics is about prioritizing individual and operational values and establishing codes of ethics and codes of conduct that ensure behaviors and internal systems are aligned with those values (Price, 2001). Many organizations have programs specifically designed to address ethical issues that their employees are required to attend. These programs encourage strong teamwork and productivity, promote ethical credibility and support employee growth, all of which not only enhance the organization's public image of ethical credibility, but also encourage the growth of diversity.

Successful leaders in any organization will give full support to implementation of formal ethics programs. This articulates a serious commitment to ethical behavior and provides clear standards for behaviors that are preferred by the organization. It also alerts employees to expected behaviors and minimizes the chances of unethical behavior occurrences.

Ethical leaders develop creative, critical thinking in their followers, provide opportunities for them to develop, welcome positive and negative feedback, recognize the contributions of others, share information with followers, and have moral standards that emphasize collective interests of the organization (Howell & Avolio, 1992). Howell and Avolio (1992) developed several key behaviors and moral standards that differentiated ethical from unethical leaders. These key factors are listed next.

> *Unethical Charismatic Leader*—Uses power only for personal gain or impact; promotes own personal vision; censures critical or opposing views demands that own decisions be accepted without question; one-way communication; insensitive to followers' needs; relies on convenient external moral standards to satisfy self-interests.
>
> *Ethical Charismatic Leader*—Uses power to service others; aligns vision with followers' needs and aspirations; considers and learns from criticism; stimulates followers to think independently and to question the leader's view; open, two-way communication; coaches, develops, and supports followers; shares recognition with others; relies on internal moral standards to satisfy organizational and societal interests.

Today's workforce places an emphasis on organizational learning and follower empowerment- conditions that promote mutual respect and dialogue (Bast, 2000). Ethical leaders are effective in that they create followers who are more capable of leading themselves and, under the guidance of ethical leaders, followers feel more independent, confident, and powerful. They eventually take responsibility for their own actions, gain rewards through self-reinforcement and, like their leader, establish a set of internal standards to guide their actions and behavior (Price, 2001).

Effective leaders have a strong moral character. In leadership, character matters, because the moral character of an organization's leaders can determine how successful that organization will be. In this day and age, morally sensitive leaders are an essential feature of any good organization. The emotional core of leadership is trust. If the leader has no morals, no values, and no virtue, then he will have no trust from his subordinates. Without a relationship of trust between leader and follower there can be no organizational success (Solomon, 1996).

Ethical leadership must, then, be effective, efficient, and excellent if it is not to waste human potential (Johnson, 2003). To be effective, efficient, and excellent the leader must understand the four basic components of ethical leadership: purpose; knowledge; authority; and trust.

- *Purpose*—The ethical leader acts with organizational purposes firmly in mind, which provides focus and consistency.
- *Knowledge*—The ethical leader has the knowledge to judge and act prudently. This knowledge is found throughout the organization and its environment, but must be shared by those who hold it.
- *Authority*—The ethical leader has the power to make decisions and act, but also recognizes that all those involved and affected must have the authority to contribute to shared purposes.
- *Trust*—The ethical leader inspires-and is the beneficiary of-trust throughout the organization and its environment. Without trust and knowledge, people are afraid to exercise their authority (Johnson, 2003).

It is also helpful to think of the ethical leader as exercising authority within five modes or levels of intervention into the judgments and actions of followers. These five modes include the items listed here.

- *Inspiration*—Setting the example so that other committed members will contribute their fullest capabilities to achieve organization purposes. This represents the lowest degree of intervention.
- *Facilitation*—Supporting other committed members, and guiding them where necessary, so that they are able to contribute their capabilities as fully as possible.
- *Persuasion*—Appealing to reason to convince other members to contribute toward achieving organizational purposes.
- *Manipulation*—Offering incentives other than the intrinsic value of contributing to the achievement of organizational purposes, where commitment is lacking.
- *Coercion*—Forcing other members to contribute some degree of their capability where they have little or no commitment to do so on their own. This represents the highest degree of intervention (Johnson, 2003).

The relationship between the four components of ethical leadership and the five modes of ethical leadership can be visualized as being interrelated and should be considered together. Attention to any one component alone is incomplete and misleading. Moreover, the style of ethical leadership will vary depending on how it reflects the organizations culture. If the culture does not support organizational learning and growth manipulative, even coercive, leadership would be exhibited (Johnson, 2003).

Declaring that ethics is at the heart of leadership, Ciulla (1995) concluded, "that a culture's ethical values are what define the concepts of leadership". Leadership is fundamental to ethical considerations (p. 2). Again, Gini (1995) avowed that

> ... without the continuous commitment, enforcement and modeling of leadership standards of business, ethics cannot and will not be achieved in organizations ... badly led [organizations] wind up doing unethical things. (p. 2)

Kouzes and Posner (1993) noted that the credibility of leadership is dependent on its moral purpose, trust, and the hopes it engendered. Effective leaders are those responsible for the moral environment of the organization, group or society, and are able to bring their followers together around common values. As leaders become more competent and morally mature, those they lead are more effective and display higher moral reasoning which usually results in success of the organization as a whole (Bass, 1997).

Leadership Styles in the Workforce

There are many different ways of leading others and the way in which one leads will determine the leadership style being used. The term *"leadership style"* refers to the manner and approach of providing direction, implementing plans, and motivating people. It is the leader's manner of behavior in a work situation (Brennen, 2002; Clark, 2000).

Currently there are four different styles of leadership that can be identified in the workforce. They include authoritarian or autocratic, participative or democratic, delegative or free reign, and bureaucratic or by the book (Brennen, 2002; Clark, 2000; Meng, 1996).

While the proper leadership style is dependent on the situation, there are many factors that influence which leadership style to use. These include the items outlined below.

- The manager's or leader's personal background. What personality, knowledge, values, ethics, and experiences does the leader have? What does he or she think will work?
- The employees being supervised. Employees are individuals with different personalities and backgrounds. The leadership style managers use will vary depending upon the individual employee and what he or she will respond to best.

- The company. The traditions, values, philosophy, and concerns of the company will influence how its leaders act (PageWise, Inc., 2002).

In the past several decades, management experts have gone from a very classical autocratic approach to a very creative, participative approach in defining leadership. But, if one were to take a close look at the differences between these styles, they would find that they are totally different in some respects, and quite similar in others (Timberlake, 2000).

Autocratic Leadership Style—This style of leadership is often considered the classical approach to leading. The leader using this style of leadership makes all the decisions and passes the directives to subordinates who are expected to carry these out under very close supervision. The leader does not consult employees nor are they allowed to give any input. As a matter of fact, any attempts by subordinates to question the directives given are discouraged. The leader retains as much power and decision-making authority as possible, which is why this style of leadership is often referred to as the "authoritarian" style. This style of leadership is based on the assumption that the leader knows everything, including what is best for the organization. Employees are considered ignorant, indolent, ambitionless, and irresponsible. They cannot be trusted to do what is right for the organization and therefore, prefer to be led (Brennen, 2002; PageWise, Inc., 2003).

Leaders using the autocratic/authoritarian style of leadership rely on threats and punishment to influence employees; don't trust employees; and do not allow for employee input (PageWise, Inc., 2003). Authoritarian leaders can be arrogant, hostile, boastful, and egotistical.

Most people are familiar with autocratic leadership and therefore have less trouble adopting this style. Furthermore, it must be said, that in spite of its weaknesses, this style of leadership is well suited for certain environments such as where there are new, untrained employees who do not know which tasks to perform or which procedures to follow; employees don't respond to any other leadership style; there is limited time in which to make decisions; there are high-volume productions needs on a daily basis; and in situations in which the lives of people depend on others following orders such as the military or a prison.

> *Bureaucratic Leadership Style*—This style of leadership is also known as the "by the book" leadership style. Leaders and managers using this style of leadership make sure all tasks are performed according to procedure and policy. If the book does not cover a specific task, then the manager refers to the next level above him for advice. This style of leadership can be effective when employees are performing routine tasks over and over; employees need to understand certain standards and procedures; working with dangerous or

delicate equipment that requires a definite set of procedures to operate; safety or security training is being conducted among others.

Drawbacks to this style of leadership include formation of work habits that are no longer useful, but are difficult to break; employees losing interest in their jobs and in their fellow workers; and employees doing only what is expected and no more (PageWise, Inc., 2002).

Democratic Leadership Style—This style of leadership is also known as the "participative" style of leadership as it encourages employees to be a part of the decision making. It focuses on group relationships and sensitivity to people in the organization. The democratic leader makes decisions by consulting his team, whilst still maintaining control of the group (Meng, 1996). Subordinates are encouraged to express their ideas and make suggestions on how a task will be tackled and who will perform which task, but the leader bears the crucial responsibility of leadership. Supervision is minimal as individuals take responsibility for their behavior. In other words, this style of leadership requires the leader to be a coach who has the final say, but gathers information from staff members before making a decision, thereby promoting employee participation and professional growth (Brennen, 2002; Clark, 2000; PageWise, Inc., 2002).

Typically the democratic leaders tend to have a warm, confident, and friendly demeanor. They develop plans to help their employees evaluate their own performance; encourage employees to grow on the job and be promoted; and recognize employee achievements which promotes team spirit, and high morale.

The democratic leadership style is most effective when used with highly skilled or experienced employees; to implement operational changes or resolving individual or group problems; the leaders wants to keep employees informed about matter that affect them; the leader wants employees to share in decision-making and problem-solving duties and; when the leader wants to provide opportunities for the employee to develop a high sense of personal growth and job satisfaction.

This style of leadership is least effective in situations where there is not enough time to get input from everyone. It is easier and more cost-effective for the manager to make the decision; the business can't afford mistakes; or when employee safety is a critical concern (PageWise, Inc., 2002).

Delegate or Laissez-Faire Leadership Style—This leadership style is also known as the "free reign" or "hands off" style of leadership. It is one in which the leader provides little or no direction or support, shows lack of caring for what followers do and often seems uninvolved or indecisive to followers. Due to the absence of any real leadership, everyone is free to do as he/she pleases (Brennen, 2002). All authority or power is given to the employees who must determine goals, make decisions, and resolve problems on their own, although the proposed leader is responsible for the decisions that are made (Clark, 2000). The term "Laissez-Faire" is a French term that means the noninterference in the affairs of others and represents a leadership style that is not usually advocated in most situations, although it has its place with employees who are highly motivated, skilled, experienced, and trustworthy. Laissez-Faire leadership also works well in situations where the employees have pride in their work and a drive to do it successfully on their own, or simply when the decisions to be made are do not significantly affect the overall operation of the organization (PageWise, Inc., 2002). Laissez-Faire leadership has often been termed "the dark side of empowerment", because the followers are given the tasks to be performed, but receive no goals or direction for performing those tasks (DiStefano, 2000; Kelly, 2000). As a result, there is a state of confusion and lack of confidence in leadership. The employees often doubt their own ability to accomplish the task at hand, resulting in negative effects for the organization, poor performance, social loafing by the followers, and a decrease in organizational productivity.

Leadership for Tomorrow

We have discussed various leadership principles and practices. We have talked about what it means to be a leader and the requirements for becoming an effective leader. We have identified numerous aspects of effective leadership and the qualities of being an effective leader. But, what does it all mean? What are the expectations for leadership in the future? What kind of leadership style will prove to be most effective for the leaders of tomorrow, and what qualities should an effective leader portray?

The desire to understand, define, and explain the essence of leadership has been the driving force for leadership researchers and scholars for most of the twentieth century. In their efforts to find an "accurate" and "precise" definition of leadership, thousands of studies have been published in the last several decades. The early explanations of effective leadership focused on a single person and his or her personal qualities and skills. Other researchers attempted to link effective leaders with specific abilities, traits, behaviors, and sources of power, or aspects of the situation in determining how a leader will be able to influence others.

Today, scholars discuss the nature of leadership in terms of the interaction among the people involved in the process: leaders and followers. Thus, leadership is not the work of a single person; rather, it can be defined as a collaborative endeavor among group members. In other words, the essence of leadership is not the leader, but the relationship between the leader, superiors, peers, and subordinates (Rost, 1993). Rost (1993), in his book *Leadership for the Twenty-First Century*, articulates a definition of leadership based on the post-industrial perspective of leadership. Rost's definition says that leadership is an influence relationship among leaders and followers who intend real changes that reflect their mutual purposes. He reminds us that in today's workforce leadership is not what leaders do. Rather, leadership is what leaders and followers do together for the overall benefit of the organization. In today's workforce, leaders operate in an environment in which power is shared with followers. No longer does a single leader have all the answers and the power to make substantial changes.

Slowly researchers, scholars and practitioners alike are giving up on the old ways of leadership, the industrial paradigm that is characterized by a top-down philosophy, where the leader is decisive, efficient, unemotional, and in total control of the decision-making process (Brumgardt, 1998). Collaboration, power sharing, facilitation, and empowerment, on the other hand, characterize the post-industrial leadership paradigm. If our goal is to prepare emerging leaders of the next century, it is imperative that our leadership programs reflect this new paradigm.

The Kellogg Foundation funded a research study conducted by the director of their Leadership Scholar Program (Matusak, 1997). Her findings suggest that critical incidents in leadership for the twenty-first century will include visioning, initiating, guiding, and encouraging with and through group relations. In addition, Matusak (1997) indicates that leadership is situational or a process that requires moving from the role of leaders to the role of follower depending on the circumstances. Finally, she identifies communication as the key to leadership, affirming that leaders must listen to what is being said as well as to what is not being said (Spaid & Parsons, 1999).

Allen et al. (1998) in *Rethinking Leadership Working Papers*, offered another description of leadership for the future. They indicate the *purpose* of leadership in the twenty-first century is the driving force, rather than the *definition* of leadership.

Therefore, recognizing the context of these changing times, we propose that the *purpose of leadership* in the twenty-first century is:

- To create a supportive environment where people can thrive, grow, and live in peace with one another;
- To promote harmony with nature and thereby provide sustainability for future generations;

- To create communities of reciprocal care and shared Responsibility—one where every person matters and each person's welfare and dignity is respected and supported. (p. 1)

These leadership experts indicate that leadership in the future will be confronted with many challenges which include: (1) Globalization; (2) Increasing stress on the environment; (3) Increasing speed and dissemination of information technology; and (4) Scientific and social change (Allen et al., 1998).

- *Globalization*—There is an increasing global consciousness in all sectors and societies of the workforce. Organizations must focus on marketing their products worldwide, instead of focusing on the United States, in order to compete in the broader economic playing field.
- *Increasing stress on the environment*—There are numerous issues related to the environment and its ability to support the world's populations in the future. Struggles between economic and environmental interests will continue to grow in the future.
- *Increasing speed and dissemination of information technology*—Mass communication has connected the world in ways unheard of fifty years ago. Today, electronic bits of information are transferred instantaneously via the Internet.
- *Scientific and social change*—Genetic engineering is just one of the scientific changes that will reshape our lives. Increasingly, there are more cures for long term illness and disease and radical changes in the way we produce and grow our food. Social changes will require new political, social, educational, and organizational structures to ensure survival for the future.

The ethical and spiritual dimensions of human beings mutually shape these four trends. They are highly interdependent and thus it is difficult to discuss them as discrete entities. Collectively, they will have a powerful effect on how we practice leadership in the future. And, as a leader within an organization, you must be able to understand these trends in order to determine how they will affect organizational contributions to society.

According to Allen et al. (1998) as these trends or challenges interact they will create a new set of implications that will have a profound effect on how we practice leadership in the future. These implications for leadership include:

1. *Increasing diversity in our daily lives:* Globalization has affected international travel, our perspective of other cultures, as well as immigration and growth of the U.S. population. This phenomenon has created a significant increase in diversity in our communities and in the workforce. As a result,

leadership practices must recognize diversity as a positive asset to the organizational workforce and to its surrounding communities.

2. *Increasing change:* Change in our society today takes place rapidly and does not usually allow enough time to respond adequately. In the future, the complexity of change events will increase requiring leadership to design, support and nurture flexible, durable organizations and groups. Furthermore, effective leaders must have a firm grasp and understanding of the system and how that change will affect the system in order to respond quickly and positively to the change events.

3. *Complexity:* As time goes on, the world becomes more and more complex and interwoven with a wide variety of resource networks. Leadership will need to pace and intuit the changing complexity of the system. Complexity challenges every individual's capacity to fully understand all systems. For this reason, complex concepts, infrastructures, and business ventures will require shared leadership, and multiple perspectives from any organization in order for it to survive in the future.

4. *Interdependence:* The dynamic trends of ecological stress, information technology, globalization and scientific and social change all demonstrate the impact of interdependence and demand a total systems approach. The implication for leadership will be to initiate and practice a systems perspective. In other words, leadership must embrace and approach change from all sides and respond positively to all its interrelated parts in order to benefit the new global society.

5. *Increasing tensions around value differences:* As organizations face increasing globalization, leadership is faced with the ethical ramifications of our organizations' decisions and how those decisions impact not just the individual organization or corporation but also the community and the world. This will require leadership be practiced with a significant ethical dimension that focuses on principles that can be accepted and sustained by every individual.

6. *Increasing gap between the rich and the poor:* As the tension of economic and natural resources between the rich and the poor continues, both individuals and nations will be affected. The widening gap will require leadership that recognizes justice and equity issues as well as economic and ecological concerns.

7. *Increasing requirement for continuous learning:* Leadership will be responsible for encouraging the speed at which individuals learn. Leadership also needs to provide opportunities for these individuals to grow and learn how continuous learning can be brought into the community or organization to help handle the complexities of globalization.

Allen et al. (1998) in *Leadership in the Twenty-First Century*, implies that to deal with the challenges of the future, a new form of leadership that is collaborative and shared will be the most successful approach in the next century.

This new leadership paradigm has been called by many names; shared; participatory; collective; collaborative; cooperative; democratic; fluid; inclusive and; relational. This new leadership paradigm should replace hierarchical leadership that served us in the past because the leadership style of the past is not well suited for the global complexity, rapid change, interdependency, and multifaceted challenges discussed above.

> In the information age, the primary challenge will be to encourage the new, better-educated workforce to be committed, self-managing and life-long learners. This "people-focused" leadership has its roots in democratic traditions. It is founded on the belief that in the complex future "answers are to be found in community" in group-centered organizations where "everyone can learn continually" (Senge, 1990) (as cited in Allen et al., 1998). Followers are being transformed into partners, co-leaders, life-long learners and collaborators.

The new leadership paradigm, therefore, is restructuring our conceptual framework of what the practice of leadership is and our understanding of what effective leaders do. It is transforming the role of "followers" and revolutionizing the design of organizations for the twenty-first century.

The process at the heart of this change includes collaboration and reciprocal leadership. Collaborative leadership is more adaptable and fluid, focusing on relationships and the needs of people. This type of leadership recognizes that no one person has the solution to the multifaceted problems that a group or organization must face. Leadership in this context requires a set of principles that empower all members to act, and employ a process that allows the collective wisdom of the entire group, organization, or corporation to surface.

Conclusions

The leaders of the future must know their core values and be able to voice them as well as the concerns of his or her followers. They must be flexible, able to relate to all constituencies, adapt well to change and be prepared for times of uncertainty. They must have leadership qualities, which are historically masculine, such as analytic thinking, control, and little emotional interaction, in addition to historically feminine leadership qualities which include collaboration, emotional and interpersonal connection (Loden, 1985) (as cited in D'Ambrosio, 2000). In other words, components of both sets of qualities reflected in masculine and feminine leadership are needed to enhance the interactive relationship between leader and follower.

In the future, leadership will have to face many new changes and challenges brought on by increasing technological advances and globalization. Leaders of the future must lead with accuracy of judgment and be able to face adaptive challenges by having a vision of the whole picture. They must be able to regulate distress in the workplace, maintain disciplined action and protect the voices of leaders below. The future of leadership lies in teamwork. No leader leads without followers. There must be a shared vision between leaders and followers of the future to guarantee organizational success. The role of the follower is equally important in the dynamic leadership process. Leaders have always had a voice but now followers do also. To have a voice means to be able to speak passionately about something (D'Ambrosio, 2000). It also includes listening to the voices from within the organization.

Leaders of the future must use the *Full Range of Leadership Model* which fosters leadership development and potential. In this model transactions are built on mutual respect and trust between leader and followers. As a result of the positive transactions, a transformational leader who is compassionate, collaborative and open to new ideas is created. This model of leadership fosters leaders who are emotionally intelligent and effective. They have a clear knowledge of ethics and values; a passion and a purpose; are proactive and committed; and exhibit self-confidence and wisdom when dealing with the challenges facing the organization they lead. Moreover, leaders and potential leaders should examine what other leaders have done in times of crisis. By looking at others' experiences, leaders can better anticipate what they should do when faced with leadership challenges. This practice teaches strategic thinking and how to act decisively.

Leadership today is multitalented, multifaceted, and multidirectional which is an excellent representation of the qualities of the contemporary society in which we live. Slowly scholars, researchers, and practitioners alike are abandoning the old ways of traditional leadership, the *industrial paradigm*. This traditional approach to leadership is characterized by a top-down philosophy, where the leader is decisive, efficient, unemotional and in-control. The new approach to leadership, the *post-industrial paradigm*, on the other hand is characterized by collaboration, power-sharing, facilitation and empowerment. Every individual, whether leader or follower, must share the responsibility of leadership to promote the success of the organization. Only when we all work together can we bring about successful changes for our mutual purposes.

Finally, a good recipe for effective leadership:

> Good leaders have 'goal directed visions' and then achieve them by 'inspiring their people' to work through change and challenges in order for 'task accomplishment.' This, in sum, equals a successful organization. (Clark, 2000)

We leave you with a quote from Jesse Jackson that sums up what it means to be a leader. "Leaders must be tough enough to fight, tender enough to cry, human enough to make mistakes, humble enough to admit them, strong enough to absorb the pain, and resilient enough to bounce back and keep on moving."

References

Allen, K. E., Bordas, J. G., Gill, R. H., Matusak, L. R., Sorenson, G. J., & Whitmire, K. J. (1998). *Leaders in the Twenty-First Century*. Retrieved March 1, 2004, from http://www.academy.umd.edu/publications/Klspdocs/21stcen.html.
Avolio, B. J., Waldman, D. A., & Yammarino, F. J. (1991). Leading in the 1990s: The Four I's of Transformational Leadership. *Journal of European Industrial Training, 15*(4), 9–16.
Barbuto, J. E., & Brown, L. L. (2000). *Full Range Leadership (NetGuide)*. University of Nebraska-Lincoln. Retrieved on April 19, 2004, from http://www.ianrpubs.unl.edu/consumered/g1406.htm.
Bass, B. M. (1989). *Stogdil's handbook of leadership: A survey of theory and research*. New York: Free Press.
Bass, B. M. (1997). The Ethics of Transformational Leadership. *Kellogg Leadership Studies Project*. Retrieved on November 5, 2003, from http://www.academy.umd.edu/publications/klspdocs/bbass_p1.htm.
Bass, B. M., & Avolio, B. J. (1999). *Training full range leadership: A resource guide for training with the MLQ*. Redwood City, CA: Mind Garden.
Bass, B. M., & Steidlmeier, P. (1998). *Ethics, character, and authentic transformational leadership*. Retrieved on November 11, 2003, from http :IIcis. binghamtom.edu/BassSteid.html.
Bast, M. R. (2000). *Out of the Box Coaching and Working With The Enneagram*. Retrieved on November 10, 2003, from http://www.breakoutofthebox.com/charisma.htm.
Blanchard, K., & Peale, N. V. (1988). *The Power of ethical management: Community College Leadership/Ethical Leadership*. New York: NY: Fawcett.
Brennen, A. M. (2002). Leadership styles. *Educational Administration & Supervision*. Retrieved on April 19, 2004, from http://www.soencouragement.org/leadershipstyles.htm.
Brungardt, C. L. (1998). *The new face of leadership: Implications for higher education*. Retrieved on March 1, 2004, from http://www.nwlink.com/donclark/leader/lead edu.html.
Burns, J. M. (1978). *Leadership*, New York: Harper & Row.
Ciulla, J. B. (1995). Leadership ethics: Mapping the territory. *Business Ethics Quarterly, 5*, 5–28.
Clark, D. (1997). *Diversity, teams, and training*. Retrieved on March 1, 2004, from http://www.nwlink.com/donclark/leader/diverse.html.
Clark, D. (2000a). *Big Dog's Leadership Page-Concept of Leadership*. Retrieved on March 1, 2004, from http://www.nwlink.com/donclark/leader/leadcon.html.
Clark, D. (2000b). *Big Dog's Leadership Page- Human Behavior*. Retrieved on March 1, 2004, from http://www.nwlink.com/donclark/leader/leadhb.html.

Clark, D. (2000c). *Big Dog's Leadership Page- Leadership Styles.* Retrieved on March 1, 2004, from http://www.nwlink.com/donclark/leader/leadstl.html.

Clark, D. (2000d). Frequently Asked Questions on Leadership. *Leader Training and Development Outline.* Retrieved on March 1, 2004. from http:*1*/www.nwlink.com/donclark/leaderfaq.html.

D'Ambrosio, M. (2000). *Leadership in Today's World.* Retrieved on February 6, 2004, from http://www.stanswartz.com/DAMBROSIO.htm.

Daresh, J. C. (2001a). Leadership. In *Supervision as proactive leadership* (pp. 104–132). Prospect Heights, IL: Waveland Press.

Daresh, J. C. (2001b). Motivation. In *Supervision as proactive leadership* (pp. 136–147). Prospect Heights, IL: Waveland Press.

Dong, I. J., & Avolio, B. J. (1999). Effects of leadership and followers' cultural orientation on performance in group and individual task conditions. *Academy of Management Journal, 42*(2), 208–218. Retrieved on February 13, 2004, from http://web5.infotrac.galegroup.com/itw/infomark/363/384/45443494w5/purl=rei GBFM.

Epitropaki, O. (2001). *What is transformational leadership?* Institute of Work Psychology, University of Sheffield, England.

Gini, A. (1995). Too much to say about something. *Business Ethics Quarterly, 5,* 143–155.

Haughey, L. (2003). Five standards of excellence practiced by ethical leaders. *Workforce Management.* Retrieved on April 20, 2004, from http://www.workforce.com/section/09/article/23/55/60printer.html.

Helgesen, S. (1995). *The web inclusion.* New York, NY: Currency, Doubleday.

Howell, J. M., & Avolio, B. J. (1992). The ethics of charismatic leadership: Submission or liberation. *Academy of Management Executive, 6*(2), 43–54. Retrieved on November 10, 2003, from http://www.breakoutofthebox.com/charisma.htm.

Johnson, K. (1999). *The role of leadership in organizational integrity, and five modes of ethical leadership.* Ethics & Policy Integration Center (Epic). Retrieved on April 20, 2004, from http://www.ethicaledge.com/quest4.html.

Kent, R. H. (2004). Guidelines for successful leadership. *The Mansis Development Corporation.* Retrieved on March 2, 2004, from http://www.mansis.com/page124.htm.

Kouzes, J. M., & Posner, B. Z. (1993). *Credibility: How leaders gain and lose it and why people demand it.* San Francisco: Jossey-Bass.

Leadership Styles. (1996). Retrieved on March 2, 2004, from http://www.see.ed.ac.uk/gerard/MENG/ME96/Documents/Styles/styles.html.

Loden, M. (1985). *Feminine leadership or how to succeed in business without being one of the boys.* New York, NY: Times Books.

Magalhaes, F. B. (2001a). Leaders and followers. *Emerging Leader.Com* Retrieved on April 24, 2004, from http://www.emergingleader.com/article13.shtml.

Magalhaes, F. B. (2001b). The Leader. *Emerging Leader.Com.* Retrieved on April 10, 2004, from http://www.emergingleader.com/article8.shtml.

Management Learing.Com (2000–2003). *James McGregor Burns.* Retrieved on May 5, 2003, from http://managementlearning.corn/ppllburnjam. html.

McCarty, L. (2001). The humble leader. *Emerging Leader.Com*, 1998–2001. Retrieved on March 24, 2004, from http://www.emergingleader.com/article20.shtml.

Munro, P., & Beeson, J. (2002). *Leadership's purpose—attaining a culture of understanding.* Paper presented at the INTERCM Conference Leadership in Museums: Are our Core Values Shifting, Dublin, Ireland, October 16–19, 2002.

PageWise, Inc. (2002). *Styles of Leadership.* Retrieved on March 2, 2004, from http://ut.essortment.com/leadershipstyle rrnq.htm.

Price, B. (2001). Values determine credibility and ethics. *Emerging Leader.Com.* Retrieved on March 24, 2004, from http://www.emergingleader.com/article27.shtml.

Reese, C. (2003). A Book Review Article {Review of the Book Leadership and the Culture of Trust}. Retrieved on March 16, 2004, from http://www.leadingtoday.org/Onmag/august03/bra-august03. Html.

Rubenstein, H. (2004). What leaders do: A checklist. *The CEO Refresher.* Retrieved on March 9, 2004, from http://www.refresher.com/!hrrchecklist.html.

Spaid, R., & Parsons, M. H. (1999, Spring). Meeting the Millennium's challenge: Leading from where you are. *New Directions for Community Colleges, 105,* 13–19.

Taylor, P. (1994). Leadership in education. *Emergency Librarian, 21*(3), 9. Retrieved on November 3, 2003, from http://weblinks2.epnet.com/DeliveryPrint.

Thomas, G. (2001a). What leadership is not. *WeLead Online Magazine.* Retrieved on November 5, 2003, from http://www.leadingtoday.org/OnmaglfebO llnoleader2200 1.htm.

Thomas, G. (2001b). Where have all the followers gone? One leader's perspective. *WeLead Online Magazine.* Retrieved on November 5, 2003, from http://www.leadingtoday.org/Onmag!juneO1/gt-juneO1.html.

Thomas, G. (2001c). Where have all the leaders gone? One leader's perspective. *weLead Online Magazine.* Retrieved on November 11, 2003, from http://www.leadingtoday.org/Onmag/mayOl/gt-mayOl.html.

Thomas, G. (2001d). What you need to know about "situational leadership"! One leader's perspective. *weLead Online Magazine.* Retrieved on November 11, 2003, from http:///www.leadingtoday.org/Onmag/augustO1/gt-augustO1.html.

Thomas, G. (2003a). What is "transactional leadership"? *weLead Online Magazine.* Retrieved on November 5, 2003, from http://www.leadingtoday.org/Onmag!jan03/transactional2003.html.

Thomas, G. (2003b). What is "transformational leadership"? *weLead Online Magazine.* Retrieved on November 5, 2003, from http://www.leadingtoday.org/Onmag/feb03/transform22003.html.

Timberlake, B. (2000). Leadership styles. Retrieved on April 19, 2004, from http://academic.emporia.edu/smithwil/00fallmg443/ejaltimber.htm.

Trott, M. C., & Windsor, K. (1999). Leadership effectiveness: how do you measure up? *Nursing Economic$, 17*(3), 127, 4p, 2 charts. Retrieved on November 18, 2003, from http://ezproxy.library.unlv.edu:2099/DeliveryPrintSave.asp?tb= l&_ug=dbs+O+1n+en us+si.

Useem, M. (2001). How to groom the leaders of the future. Retrieved on November 5, 2003, from http://www.leadingtoday.org/Onmagl]ulyOllmu-julyOI.html.

Webster's II New College Dictionary. (1995). *Riverside University Dictionary*, PE 1628. Boston, NY: Houghton Mifflin Company.

weLead Onling Magazine. (2001). *8 Traits of Effective Leaders and Leadership Self-discovery*. Retrieved on November 11, 2003, from http://www.leadingtoday.org/Onmag/marchO1/leadertraits.html.

Wolfson, B. J. (2002). It's true lead and they will follow. *Center for Simplified Strategic Planning, Inc.* Retrieved on March 9, 2004, from http://www.strategyletter.com/CD0602/featured article.html.

W. K. Kellogg Foundation. (2003, July 2–9). *Capitalizing on our differences: Leadership across cultural boundaries and geographic borders in a global society.* Retrieved March 16, 2004, from http://www.leadershiponlinewkkforg/acrossdifferences/index.asp.

Zust, C. W. (2001a). Baby boomer leaders face challenges communicating across generations. *Emerging Leader.Com.* Retrieved on March 24, 2004, from http://www.emergingleader.com/article16.shtml.

Zust, C. W. (2001b). The best leaders know when to follow. *Emerging Leader.Com.* Retrieved on March 24, 2004, from http://www.emergingleader.com/article28.shtml.

CHAPTER TWO

I REMEMBER MAMA SAID ... (The Black Male Leader, His Attitudes, Motivation, and Instruction)

ALPHONSO SIMPSON, JR, PhD

"All that I am and ever hope to be, I owe to my angel mother."
—Abraham Lincoln

As I began to ponder the thought of writing about leadership and my space within the confines of it, I remember looking through a book of poetry earlier in the week and I came across this poem. While reflecting on Maya Angelou's poem "On Aging", I immediately thought of my place in leadership and the nurtured encouragement I got from my mama. Mama ... the name so many men of color can attach to power, strength, fortitude, courage, endurance, and comfort. Mama ... that name held a lot of weight and power for many of us. It was as if the word (or for many of us, the name) mama could solve a million problems. We called on mama in the midst of trouble as children. For instance, when the neighbors big black and tan German Shepherd got loose and decided to chase kids up trees, onto the tops of cars or into the house altogether, the magic word that seemed to give you some sort of super power to get you to safety before that dog got to you was "mama". When you found yourself against mama's will riding the new bike you just got for your birthday down the biggest hill in town, because all the older kids were doing it and your handlebars began to shake uncontrollably as you saw sketches from your short life flash before you in the concrete below, the name you called in the midst of that calamity brought on by sheer hard-headedness and pride was "mama". Mama—the "name above all names", the name that held power beyond belief for countless black children. It was the main ingredient in the grade school "do right" potion. "I'm telling your mama", the teacher would say and suddenly, because you believed her, not only did everything change, but the atmosphere shifted and you almost felt like the proverbial scarlet letter was attached to your chest for the rest of the school day because even your so-called best friends tried to stay away from you because they didn't want the threat of "I'm telling your mama too" used against them for even being remotely associated with you for the rest of the day. When that name was used against you in the midst of a reprimand, it was like a reset button that would automatically help you "slow-your-row" as we would say back at home in Andalusia, Alabama. Mama—the cause and cure for it all.

With the help and guidance of mama's hands, our experiences as black men are vast, and the baggage with which we as men of color enter upon countless life lessons setting us up on a path to leadership vary as much as our experiences do. But, in one respect, we men are all very much alike—we have all had various experiences of leadership in one way or another and regardless of color, by nature of our birth status, often times we think we have it all together and know exactly what it is like to lead. In other words, we can be quite stubborn to simple instruction as men. While we bring countless levels of experience in leadership to the table, they manifest in many forms throughout our lives; confidence reservation, narrow-mindedness, profundity, chauvinism, pride, shame, and the list goes on. In all cases, we've come to expect from these leadership experiences exactly what we've found good to hold on to in past learning and leadership situations; and given our unique personality mixes, leading as men of color has either been stressful, anxiety-producing, worrisome and demanding, or relaxing, enjoyable, fulfilling and in some cases therapeutic or an amalgam of both.

The leadership positions of Black males in the United States are very complex and peculiar. Spanning the high point of slavery to the advent of the twenty-first century, Black Males have been in an unremitting struggle to gain a sense of independence separate from the confines of the institution. Be it the institutions of slavery, organized religion, marriage, or even higher education, as leaders, black men have sought to make a name for themselves and not just settle for the names and the spaces that have been carved out and created for them. With this thought, for scores of black men, leadership has not come straightforwardly. It has been an uphill journey with many miles still ahead. Though there have been numerous markers of encouragement along the way, the climb has been steady and rough.

The election of the nation's first black President back in 2009 was something many of us never thought we would see in our lifetime. As young black scholars, we knew it was bound to happen, we just did not expect it to take place so quickly.

Barak Obama's election and presidency has taught us many things, but one thing in particular stands out to me as I fashion this piece, and it is this; the necessity for not only positive leaders and role models, but mentorship and guidance in leadership along with those who will stand as exemplars of the same is excessive in the heart of the black community. Though we had a Commander in Chief of African origin, Black males in this country have been and are currently being misunderstood, mis-educated, mis-socialized, misrepresented, misdiagnosed, and mistaken on myriad levels. Not only that, but our society as a whole seems to be blind to the fact that this is an ever present problem here in America and while the leader of our nation was a Black man, he is just that—ONE BLACK MAN. He is one Black man in a very pre-judgmental European-dominated society that perpetually feeds on an illusion of the successful black male image. While the image of the successful black man in America is certainly a reality to some, for many that image is only an illusion that acts as a double edged sword whose blade cuts both wide and deep and has done much more damage to the real black male image than any lynch mob could have ever done. The guise of the successful black male has misled many young black males for decades and even in the center of what seems to be forward progression in Black America, we have somehow been marketed, bought, pre-packaged, and re-sold for a different use today. How did we ever get to this place? How did we ever allow ourselves to be peddled like this? Observing the institution from the root, not only does this cultural transaction of being "sold" take place in just the mainstream, it actually commenced in what I like to call the academic marketplace. This concept implies that African Americans (males in particular) have been, and are currently looked at in this country as products or commodities, from the moment the first African captive touched soil on this land to the present day.

The oppressive nature of the dominant culture is so pervasive and insidious as far as the Black male and his supposedly daunting characteristics and attributes are concerned. Over time, his life, purpose, and value have been systematically diminished to a dollar amount, so much so that by the time he finally wakes up and realizes that he has been suited for sale, he has already been through a process of being washed, scrubbed, polished, packaged, and shipped. So it is here that the black male is dropped off into a whole new world that has multiple expectations for him. Expectations so low that there is no challenge set before him allowing his to flourish and grow, or expectations so high that failure is predicted and justified by the architects of this obscure sociopolitical system we call American education.

Barack Obama is a great man, was an outstanding President and a top-notch leader, however he can only do so much. The bulk of the responsibility falls on the shoulders of those of us who consider ourselves to be the common, ordinary folk who work hard and honest, who pay it forward, who are not afraid to commit and follow through. The responsibility falls on the shoulders of those of us who serve in the capacity of leadership within our homes, schools, churches, and jobs.

> I AM A LEADER ...
> I AM A BLACK MALE ...
> I AM A BLACK MALE IN LEADERSHIP ...
> I AM IN CHARGE ...

I found myself brainstorming about this manuscript standing behind a cash register in the concession stand of a local movie theater scooping bags of popcorn. What was I, of all people, doing standing behind a cash register selling popcorn? Why am I not sitting behind that big glass-topped solid oak desk in my office on campus or tucked away in my man-cave/office at home babysitting a nice large cup of black coffee? Because I am a leader. I have to make ends meet. I am charged to bring possibility to impossibility. I must lead by example. I have to take the low road for a while. I get in the trenches. I humble myself and sharpen my ability to become all things to all people. I lead because I must. I was created to lead ... at least that is what I believe. Besides, many years ago, my mama said I was.

Before I continue, I have a confession to make. Confession is good for the soul so they say. Well, my paternal grandmother was a principal. My daddy, before he retired taught elementary school. My mama, who has retired and gone back to teaching, teaches middle school. My sister, who is still teaching, has taught both middle school and high school, and to bring up the rear in this long line of educational leadership within my family. I am a fully tenured college professor (here goes the confession) who has very little faith left in what we call Higher Education. What could I possibly mean by that you might ask? Well, throughout my tenure, I have been exposed to the darker side of the "academic" game and the political infrastructure that makes it possible for the haves and the have nots to keep a very thin line of demarcation between them while maintaining a constant press toward an imaginary middle to keep each other pacified. This Neverland of what I once saw as the true and living world of Higher Education was, all along, only a mirage. Don't get me wrong, from the beginning, I felt as thought I had found a career path that would lead to many years of stability and satisfaction. In the Spring of 2000, I had arrived. I had completed the marathon, the hooding ceremony was complete and I was Dr. Alphonso Simpson, Jr., a young 27-year old Ph.D. with a very bright future ahead. I had already been hired at a state university and everything was steady. Then, one morning thirteen years and two promotions later over an invited cup of coffee of which I was told to "grab the cup that matched my tie", it all came tumbling down like a top-heavy bookshelf loaded with aluminum cans of festered buzzard eggs and bullshit consciously mixed together. "Well, you've done a fantastic job these past three years as interim department chair. You've taken your department higher than it has ever gone. The students adore you and they love what you have brought to the table. With that said, the enrollment has grown tremendously under your leadership and the numbers are constantly rising. Students are taking an interest in African American Studies like never before. Mentoring and successfully getting ten undergraduate students accepted to present at a National Conference to which you drove them to Atlanta was not only noteworthy, but an act of service that spoke volumes to your ability to lead. You really have brought greater visibility to the College of Arts and Sciences through what African American Studies has accomplished over the past three years. Not to mention You've written two books during this time and picked up some of the slack within the department teaching load despite maintaining your 3 courses even as an administrator during some really tough times for a fellow colleague in the department who had to take an emergency leave of absence for the remainder of the a semester. Dr. Simpson, your faculty members really like you and are all very supportive. You have really been an asset to the department and the college as a whole, but we believe we want to see the department go in a different direction". There it was … the crash, bang, boom that catapulted me into a particular role of leadership that seemed to fall upon me like the initial stages of the common cold.

My mama used to say "Son, sometimes the only way up is down." Well, down I was and the path of servant leadership had been carved out before my very eyes for only me to behold. I did not see it then and to be honest, I'm not so sure I see it so clearly now. I am still learning the way, even though I have made some drastically wrong turns, run into a few brick walls and fallen into a number of pits seen and unseen. As I find myself writing this monograph, broken pieces of who I have become are being revealed to me that are not only empowering as I reflect upon my contribution to the larger picture, but also painfully assuring that even on this stretch of rocky terrain, all things are somehow working together for my good. Now as hard as that was to write, I really do believe it. I have just enough faith to honestly believe that everything is working together for my good even though my current circumstances on the swiftly tilting planet of Higher Education are not very re-assuring for me. "Everything" (as mama would say) "is working as it should just for my good". In actuality, her words were "Aww honey, It'll be alright. Just you wait and see." She also used to tell me when it came to understanding people, their idiosyncrasies and the things that have been aligned for us throughout various stages of life that if I kept my faith in what God has pre-designed specifically for me that everything would work out in my favor. She would remind me quite often that faith doesn't make sense and likewise, sense doesn't make faith so "stop trying to make sense out of a faith-walk" she would say.

In the process of bringing forth this piece theoretically, I contemplated on how I would present my work in a manner that was personal, yet metaphorical and understandable. As I thought about the method I would choose to utilize throughout this writing process, I began to consider the various steps an artist would use since I really wanted to create a piece of work through words that would paint a vivid picture of myself, my experiences, and my mama. Taking what I had to work with, I chose to focus on the various steps an artist would take in order to bring a portrait into fruition. As I often times do when I'm in an awkward headspace, I phoned my mama who is a seasoned artist herself. Once we got all of the small talk out of the way, I was able to ask about the steps one would take in order to paint a portrait. She began to explain in a rather sarcastic but assuring manner that one would first need to find a subject to feature. She proceeded to say, "After you have chosen a subject for your painting, you need to choose the size and type of surface you want to use as your canvas. When I say canvas, I am talking about what you would actually paint the portrait on to." She didn't know it at the time, but she told me something rather deep at this point. She said "different surfaces yield different results. If I chose to paint on burlap rather than on felt, the portrait would have a different texture, and a different look all together after I finished it, so your surface choice is very important." She went on to say, "After you have decided on what type of surface you want to use for the painting, you will need to illuminate the canvas or cover it with a thin layer of Gesso." Of course, me not being an artist in this regard, I asked "What is Gesso mama?" She said, "Oh honey, Gesso is a medium that you put on any canvas. It makes the surface pliable so that the paint will stay on it." She went on to say, "The application of gesso is a very important step in painting any portrait because you want your work to last." Another golden nugget of insight she had given unbeknown to her! Mama didn't know it, but she was revealing so much to me on a much deeper level than she had ever intended. I was outdone. She kept going as she added "This illumination of your canvas will assure you that the paints you apply will stay once you have them on your canvas. After you have taken the time to paint the portrait, it is of utmost importance that you critique it before anyone else does. In critiquing your portrait, you look for flaws and holes in the work. You are looking back and reflecting on what you have created as well as how you created it to make sure that it is in good taste." Mama was knocking it out of the park for me this night! She proceeded to tell me that my work "had to be something that was pleasing to me as the artist as well as to my audience." She said, "The people who make up your audience will always be your biggest critics." She also said "Son, whatever you do, make sure that when all is said and done, you like what you have created. It is equally important that your critics respect your work; however, you have to accept, respect, and admire your own work before anyone else does. You need to be satisfied with it first because after all, you created it, you are the person solely responsible for its actuality." Mama did it for me that night! Her comments to me were so relevant as the word artist I sought to be. I was so grateful for her insight even though she had no idea that I was making transfers and connections to draw a parallel between writing and painting. Mama was on a roll at this point about painting as she gave me one more piece of advice that blew this whole concept out of the water for me. She said "oh yeah, baby, once you are completely satisfied with the painting, it is important that you highlight and bring out certain elements in it." She then asked me "What do you do after you are done with a picture that you have created and really like?" Me, trying to be deep said with an air of confidence "Umm, you hang it up for everybody to see." She said, "Now you know better than that Brother"(that's my nickname), she said "You've finished your painting but it's not really complete until you frame it." That was so profound! "Once you have found the proper type of frame, it will compliment every important detail in the portrait. You want to be sure that your frame is not too simple, nor too flamboyant." She said "You know people say that a picture is worth a thousand words, however, we artist like to say that if a picture is worth a thousand words, then the right frame has to be worth at least-ten thousand words. In essence, your portrait may be great in and of itself, however, the wrong frame can greatly devalue it. Son, make sure that you take your time and choose the best frame for the work you have created." I am not sure if mama knew that she was giving me some good sound life skill advice or if she thought she was simply giving me the "abcs" of portrait painting. Nevertheless, the conversation we had that evening over the phone put so much into perspective for me.

Mrs. Addie R. Simpson is the ultimate teacher. Everyone who knows my mama knows that she is married to the profession of teaching. When I say, "married", I mean that in a very kind and loving way. As I called home on another evening to ask her if she thought it rude to say that she was "married" to the profession of teaching, she chuckled a little and said "Son, your mama's first love is your daddy and I'm only married to him." I knew that, of course but when it comes to teaching, my mama is defined by it. Yes, everyone knows her as Paula and Brother's mama second, and Coach Simpson's wife first, but even more people know her as Mrs. Simpson, the middle school Art teacher. Not one person who has gone through the Andalusia public school system over the past 40+ years can say that they have never had a Mrs. Simpson middle school art project sitting somewhere in their house at one point in their life. Almost every home in Andalusia has had or still has a piece of art somewhere that has my mama's signature etched somewhere on it. Whether it was an ashtray, a clay pot, a ceramic mold of a mallard duck or a happy/sad clown, a stringed art picture, a wood-burned piece or the all too famous 6th grade yarn dog, most everybody who passed through Andalusia City Schools took something home from room 24 between the 6th and 8th grade.

My mama taught me to lead by her example. She was and still is a very committed educator who personifies servant leadership. Mama has always put others first in regard to leading. I really believe that she has embodied the Scripture in Matthew 23:11 that says "But he that is greatest among you shall be your servant." Even though the middle school has moved to a different set of buildings over on another campus across town, that corner room (room 24) over by the tennis courts at Andalusia Middle School in Andalusia, Alabama will forever be mama's art room to me. The images are vivid in my mind. I see them as if I were watching my favorite movie for the millionth time. I can also recall the distinct smells of fresh plaster of Paris, baked pottery, speckled glazes used for decorating 7th grade bowls and vases made of coiled clay, and the pungent but pleasant aroma of those hot wood-burning pens as they were pressed against cross-sections of pine tree wood. Most vividly, I can recall the image of that Canary yellow door to mama's art storage room that had these words painted on it in her handwriting:

> *Accept Me, I am I*
> *Do not change me,*
> *Condemn me,*
> *Nor put me down.*
> *Perfect, I may never be,*
> *So, do not insult me nor make me feel unhappy,*
> *I am I, and I enjoy being what I am—ME*

My sister and I, upon entering mama's art room, would race to see who could recite that poem on the storage room door the fastest. After teasing each other about losing and not having it memorized, we would then move over to the section of her room that had a picture of a fisherman painted on the wall next to the storage room. There was another quote that sort of fashioned a portion of not only the teaching philosophy that I would soon adopt, but also my life as a man. The quote said:

> "If you give a man a fish,
> he will eat for a day,
> But, if you teach a man to fish,
> he will eat for a lifetime."

Yes, mama's room holds several memories for me. As I reflect, even as a student in her 6th, 7th, and 8th grade classes, (I took art every year) I remember so many incidents, conversations, and life lessons that shaped and molded me into the man, the husband, the father, the scholar, musician, friend, and servant leader that I have become. Mama has always been a driving force for me. She has stood as a point of reference for almost everything I have encountered. Within her character was patience beyond expectation for the age group of children who think they know it all. She was the bastion of patience in my opinion back during those days. I don't know if it was just for me, but I never saw my mama lose herself in her classroom even in the heat of catty female scuffles and male ego challenges. Mama said, "Son, you never let someone else make you lose your mind, especially in a place where you have jurisdictional government." I had no idea what that meant at that time, but as I found myself pushed to the limit a time or two in the post-secondary classroom, I could hear her saying "you have jurisdictional government in here, this is YOUR room. Don't you ever let students push you to where you can't keep yourself, because at the end of the day, you are in charge."

Mama's art room was not the only scene of my leadership forming years. I can vividly recall several evenings riding to Libertyville, Alabama with mama as co-pilot to Mrs. Grissett's Art Studio. Libertyville was a small community on the outskirts of town on highway 55 that would take you right to the Florida line. I don't think anybody lived in Libertyville but Mrs. Grissett. At any rate, this is where mama, taught me some of the greatest lessons I would ever learn in patience. As a Servant Leader, I have come to the realization that an exercise in patience somewhere along the road to leadership is essential. Sometimes we would be at that studio for at least two hours. Mama would keep me out there in Libertyville stuck in the front seat of that what seemed to be 18ft. beige and tan Caprice Classic Station Wagon with the paneling on the sides. It seemed like an eternity was spent sitting, and waiting, and sitting, and waiting, and just sitting and waiting some more. Mama would eventually come out of the Art studio sometimes with a few clay molds, some paint, a few blocks of clay and maybe a canvas or two after which she would say very matter-of-factly to me "We're gonna just drop this by the art room before we go home okay?" Me, being a mama's boy would say "okay" and just ride in that front seat wondering to what all of this would lead to for me. What exactly was this accomplishing in my life beside killing time? I did not know it, until recently, that my mama did those things and took me along with her to understand dedication, commitment, and follow through. Sure she was tired, but she had a job to do and she was going to make sure that as long as her name was attached to that art program at the middle school that it would be top notch and closest to the best, if not the best in the surrounding school districts.

On several occasions I would ask myself, what would mama say about this, or what would mama think about that. Even though I have not lived as a resident under my mama and daddy's roof since the day I left for pre-drill band camp at Alabama State University in the Fall of 1991, I still, sometimes find myself thinking, "Oh, if this got back to mama …" There were things I did that I knew she would disapprove of and then again there were things I did that I am certain she would have held her head high as she proudly proclaimed "that's my son." I am blessed to have a mama who has been with me from my first breath until now. Every major milestone in my life, mama has been a part of it and for that I am extremely grateful. From the very first day of kindergarten to my Doctoral hooding ceremony at the University of Wyoming in Laramie, both mama and daddy were there. Not to put my father in the shadows of my accomplishments because his presence was integral, but for every man, having mama there to share that sense of pride, having mama there to give a non-discreet nod of approval, to have mama there to clap and cheer louder than anyone, to have mama there to give that assuring hug that only a mama can, just to have mama there to introduce to anybody as "my mama" means the world to us men. Our mamas donned many of us with leadership roles from the very beginning when she knelt down, straightened our tie or buttoned our shirt and looked us square in the eye and said "now go make mama proud" as we were nervous about entering middle school, or crossing that high school graduation stage. To do just that … to make mama proud is that gas that fills my leadership tank. To succeed in order to see mama bask in pride and to watch her glow in admiration makes growing in leadership worth it all. Of all my recollections, I cannot seem to recall a time when mama was off putting to me, no matter how ridiculous my dreams and aspirations were. She taught me to bream big and to reach even bigger. She raised me to lead in every aspect of my life. Whenever I messed up—as I oftentimes did growing up, mama, knowing my blunder, would ask me why. That was always the million-dollar question, and when I would begin to give what I have come to know now as an excuse, she would always say, "Excuses are the tools of incompetence used to build monuments of nothing and bridges that lead to nowhere. Those who always utilize those tools seldom amount to anything son." My mama pledged Zeta Phi Beta Sorority, Inc. at Alabama State University in the early 1960s and it wasn't until I pledged Alpha Phi Alpha, Fraternity Inc., in 1995 that I really began to understand what she meant by this. I also realized when, where, and how she gained this nugget of wisdom passed on to my sister and I during our teenage years (my sister and I still joke to this day that mama was a master hazer when we were growing up—and I'm going to leave it at that). My mama named me after my father, a great man who has always lead our household in numerus ways. To me, my daddy knew everything! My daddy taught me to always have an answer—not an excuse. My mama taught me how to apply it. My parents are the best! I pray that my wife and I can someday lead our family and be half the parents my parents are to my sister and me. I know that our children (we have two daughters), will someday look back at their experiences as they are being brought up in a household that is not foreign to leadership and have as many stories, if not more about their childhood as I have. No matter what, I take comfort in knowing that our girls get some of the same teachings and nuggets of wisdom and leadership instilled into them almost every summer as they go "back home" to Andalusia to spend a number of weeks with their "Granny and Grand-daddy." Even now, my daughters have some "I remember Granny said" stories that will go with them for the rest of their lives. These are the things I live for. To know that the lessons in leadership that made me the man I am are being preserved deep within my children. I know in my heart of hearts that these lessons have been planted to be passed on throughout future generations. The messages are timeless; they can't be dated. My mama's life lessons in leadership defy the laws of mathematics as they multiply by simply dividing. By taking bits and pieces of this "do" and that "don't" have been able to weave a fabric of my own that has clothed me in humility, security, confidence, faith, integrity, and goodness. Yes, Mama's thread runs throughout my quilt of life, piecing together every experience—good or bad. In this quilt, knots are tight, patterns are intricate and, more than anything, every stitch is intentional. It's mine and it covers me, it warms me, it protects me, and gives me strength when I get to feeling like I can't make it another day.

If the characteristics of leadership were personified as my mama walked, talked and lived it, as I journey back through nearly 43 years of life, I remember hearing it say "Live right, because right ain't wrong and ain't nothing wrong with right." It would say "Don't just do good for people son, be good to people." It would also tell me, "If you take care of the tools I have given you son, your tools will in turn take care of you" and so here I am, walking into my destiny. This is my season, it is my turn now ... Mama said it was. So, I lead because I was designed to lead, there is no other way for me at this juncture in my life. I do what I know to be right and I sit back patiently and watch the benefits of servant leadership and the goodness my Mama instilled into me blossom into some of the most succulent and low hanging fruit that I could ever hope to eat. Though the process of coming into myself as a leader has been slow but steady, I have come to realize that Mama knew exactly what she was doing all along. She knew what she was working into me, as she would call me out of bed the minute I had gotten comfortable just to turn the front porch light off. She saw much further down the road for me than I ever could, and though at times it seemed like the things she did and said would be so frustrating, I have come to realize that she was playing a game of hide and seek with my future and the good things, nuggets of wisdom and strength that she had for me as her baby boy. For Mama, it was all in the timing of things. I remember one time, Mama said "I don't play games. You ain't ever got to worry about Mama playing games baby, that's something I ain't never been good at. I don't like em'. I never have and I never will." She said "Some things you just gotta wait on, they will come in their own timing, learn how to be patient, you don't want to mess up something good by being impatient". Mama was right. There again she was planting seeds that would germinate and grow for my benefit—for the benefit of my children, and their children, and their children's children. Mama knew what she was doing. There was intentionality in every "No, not right now" even in every "Because I'm the Mama and I said so" intentionality was integral to the design. I see it now! Through the eyes of a leader, I most certainly see what my mama was doing. While sometimes I thought she was just being mean, and downright unfair, she was simply preserving for such a time as this. She was right. She didn't play games. She never hid anything from me; she hid things away for me—for such a time as this so I could lead as I was supposed to. **I AM IN CHARGE NOW.**

CHAPTER THREE

A Call to Lead

GEORGES C. BENJAMIN, MD, ScD(hc)MACP, FACEP(E), FNAPA, Hon FRESPH, Hon FFFP

> *"Man's greatness consists in his ability to do and the proper application of his powers to things needed to be done."*
> —FREDERICK DOUGLASS

I have always believed that being in charge and leadership are two separate things. Many people have the opportunity to be in charge but it is not the same as leadership. Many leaders are not the people in charge. Leadership is often about being an influencer and direction driver. I have had the unique benefit of being both a leader and an influencer across a range of life experiences. A lot of what has crafted my beliefs and directions come from my life experiences and as a lifelong learner, my approach to leadership is still evolving.

Birth and Early Childhood

I was born in Chicago, Illinois, on September 28, 1952, to George and Tessie Benjamin. My parents, both from middle class families, believed strongly in education. My mother grew up in North Chicago, Illinois. Neither of her parents had much formal schooling but all of her siblings went on to seek formal education. Mom was a graduate of Waukegan Township High School, receiving her Bachelor of Science from George Williams College and later her Master of Arts, from Roosevelt University. She was a member of the Alpha Kappa Alpha Sorority. Her early career included work at Abraham Lincoln Center as a settlement house worker; as probation officer for the juvenile court of Cook County, Illinois; and as a teacher/counselor at Calumet High School on Chicago's South Side. She was a lifelong mentor to the young men and women who were assigned to her and to numerous others who just stopped in our home for help. She was a founding inspiration in my desire to help others. She passed away in 2008, at the age of 88.

My father was born in Garnett, Kansas, to a railroad worker. He was raised by family friends in California, where he attended San Jose High School and later, Bakersfield College. He received his bachelors and then came to Chicago where he attended George Williams College and received his master's degree. It was there he met my mother. He was a boys' group secretary for the YMCA for many years and then went to work for the Illinois Department of Public Aid as a social worker. My father's persistence, hard work and the numerous life lessons he shared with me as I grew up were formative in my growth and development. He emphasized hard work, honesty and owning up to your mistakes. Like my mother, there was an expectation that I would go to college and that I could be anything I wanted to be. My mother had one exception; she did not want us to be prize-fighters. She had real concerns about the head trauma and its effects from boxing. She had apparently known several people in the sport and this was her one caution. Everything else was on the table from a career perspective. Through my parents I grew up in a culture of caring for others and thinking about ways to solve broad societal problems.

My brother Michael Owen Benjamin was born September 2, 1954, in Chicago. Michael was a 1971 graduate of Calumet High School and a 1975 graduate of the University of Illinois at Urbana where he majored in music education. He later completed graduate studies at Chicago State University where he earned a master's degree in education with a concentration in special education. Michael loved music and teaching, and he dedicated his working life to teaching children with special needs. Like millions of people he struggled with mental illness, which complicated his life's work and his overall health. Despite this challenge, he lived a full and compassionate life in the community he loved, with people he loved. Michael died in 2013, in Chicago. He was 58 years old. Michael lived semi independently with my parents throughout his post college life and provided support for my mother when my father died. He then lived an independent life with some external family support. He taught me about the challenges of having a mental illness and a lot about the dignity of self-independence. He was a model for me as I later worked to move people with mental illness from large institutional settings into smaller community based housing. He remains one of my role models.

I had one other younger brother, John Albert Benjamin, who died as a teenager from bacterial meningitis. Johnny suffered from sickle cell anemia prior to the days when we gave individuals routine prophylaxis with penicillin to prevent bacterial meningitis. My interest in his disease prompted an early interest in the molecular basis of disease, which eventually drove my decision to seek a career in research and then later in medicine. Dignity and persistence while living with a severe illness was something I learned from Johnny.

I was born in the projects on the South Side of Chicago but I have very little memory of living there as we only lived there briefly. So like many African Americans in Chicago at that time, I lived in the "projects" but it played no formidable role in my life experience or decision-making. When I was about two years old, we moved to a small two-bedroom home on Chicago's South Side. These were formative years in that I have always seen myself as being raised in a middle class family. We also always had an adult around when my brothers and I were home because my brother Johnny required support from either my mother or a full-time caretaker whenever my mother worked. Because of this, I missed out on the latch key experience of many of my childhood friends.

Because of my father's job at the YMCA we spent several summers at YMCA camp. I learned a lot of team sporting skills and self-reliance skills going camping. One of the most important things I learned as a child was to work and play well with others. Some of this was reinforced during the summers I spent in vacation Bible school and later during my days as a Cub Scout.

I attended Bass Elementary School from kindergarten through sixth grade. During grammar school I spent a lot of time in one of two museums: the Museum of Science and Industry and The Field Museum of Natural History. Both were places of wonder and interest. I had the usual childhood boy toys including erector sets, chemistry sets, balls and bats. I once placed first at the elementary school science fair with an exhibit on the physiological effects of scuba diving. I learned a martial art—Judo—and eventually earned a purple belt. The martial arts teach one to be patient and to live a defensive lifestyle, not an offensive one. It also teaches methods to divert the violence perpetrated by others as a mechanism of self-defense. I had two important leadership roles during elementary school: one included being a school crossing guard and the other as a hall monitor. These helped me learn to look out for others, be more responsible and further develop a positive self-esteem. I believe that early life experiences such as this helped me develop traits that were useful later as I became a teen where there are enormous challenges around risky behavior.

I went to middle school for 7th and 8th grade at Juliette G. Low Elementary School, named for the founder of the Girl Scouts. During middle school, I was an average student. I participated in the school science fair and I joined the band

and learned to play the trombone. This began a long-time interest with music performance, which continues today. Other outside interests included expanding my martial arts experience by adding karate. I also joined the Patriots Drum and Bugle Corps at St. Brenden's Parish on the South Side. The Patriots, an African American junior drum and bugle corps, marched competitively both regionally and eventually nationally. We were a B-level corps, which meant we were a feeder for the top corps (A-corps) in the Chicagoland area. Chicago hosted some of the world's best junior drum and bugle corps. A junior drum corps was one that included youth under age 21. I played first baritone bugle and eventually became the drum major of the corps. The drum major served as the corps leader and top musical and marching director on the field. I stayed with the Patriots until summer 1968 when I joined the Vanguard Drum and Bugle Corps as a bugler; an "A" level corps from Des Plaines, Illinois, that had just won the Veterans of Foreign Wars World Championship. I learned lots of leadership lessons during my time as the Patriots' drum major. We had wins and losses on the field and since this was a relatively new organization, lots of organizational growing pains. My transition from line musician to musical leader was foundational in my understanding of how to be "one of the boys" and still provide leadership when I stepped out of the line to be the corps leader. I learned that the expectations of you as a leader do not change when you are in front of the group or in the line. In fact, it raises people's expectations of you. This is a life lesson for those aspiring leaders in waiting.

I attended Lindblom Technical High School. Lindblom was the college preparatory magnet school for students on the South Side of Chicago. It required an entrance examination to be admitted. At Lindblom, I was an average student but always expected to go to college. Unlike many students, I had no focus on where I wanted to go, but I knew I wanted to be a "scientist" probably in the field of biology. I did not have a mentor in high school and frankly had no one to guide me in my choices. The high school counselors at Lindblom were not very engaged unless you were one of the schools top performers. On the other hand, I had a lot of support from my high school music teacher, my ROTC instructors and my middle school music teacher for my interest in music and the military. These gentlemen were instrumental in my development because of their confidence in me as a leader.

During high school, I again entered the science fair with a project about the chemical transfer of learning. This was an interesting theory about using genetic material to transfer knowledge. It did not go anywhere but it started my interest in molecular genetics. I continued my interest in music by joining the band and playing first chair trombone and baritone horn. I became the manager of the band and later its drum major. The role as manager included several organizational tasks to support the school band program. As a student conductor, I helped the band during practices and as the field leader during marching band performances.

My leadership experience in ROTC was formative in many ways. I eventually rose to be a member of the cadet corps staff and a cadet major. I was the commander of the rifle drill team and, during my senior year, was honored to be selected a member of the all city cadet corps. The all city ROTC cadet corps is an honorific group of ROTC students who are selected based on a written and oral exam. That year my brother Michael was also selected from his high school and we became the first brothers to be recognized for this high honor.

I went to the Illinois Institute of Technology (IIT) for my undergraduate studies. I was liberal arts major with a concentration in biology. I joined the Navy ROTC program at IIT and was a member of the corps for two years. I left because I was unsure about my career path and felt entering the Navy would limit my options. Funny, because several months later, as I decided to pursue a career in medical research and later medical school, the military became the launching pad to my future. I never had any thoughts of being a physician but I had always known I wanted to be some kind of a scientist. While at IIT, I was working in one of my professor's labs, who was an MD, PhD. He was working on sickle cell anemia research. His work included looking to identify small molecules that would interact with the hemoglobin molecule and disrupt the sickling process. The hope was to find an anti-sickling agent that would be tolerated physiologically as a treatment for or as a mitigating agent to prevent red cell sickling. I served as his lab assistant conducting experiments to identify such an agent. It was very interesting work but in many ways frustrating because I felt I had inadequate knowledge of clinically relevant basic sciences. I felt I needed to know more to be successful in the work I was doing. I discussed this problem with a very close friend who suggested I go to medical school. She told me that the first two years would give me the required background in the biological and medical sciences that would allow me to do the kind of research I said I wanted to do. As I looked into this, it became clear that it would serve my purposes and I decided to go to medical school. Of course medical school is expensive and as I researched ways to pay for it, I found the federal Health Professions Scholarship Program (HPSP). The HPSP is an amazing program that paid tuition and fees, books and supplies and equipment for all four years. It also paid a stipend of $400 a month, which was tax-free. HPSP requires you to serve in the uniformed services to repay the scholarship. I applied for both medical school and the scholarship and received both. So it was back into uniform for me, but this time in the U.S. Army Reserves.

I was accepted at the University of Illinois, College of Medicine through their minority opportunities program. That is code for their affirmative action program.

The University of Illinois was firmly committed to increasing the number of under-represented minorities. I did my first year in a new program at the University of Illinois at Champaign—Urbana campus in downstate Illinois. This program was designed to teach the medical sciences from a problem-based approach and covered the first two years of basic sciences into one year. In addition, we saw patients our first year. This was immersion at its fullest and I discovered I was a visual person from a learning perspective. Being able to put the basic sciences into context and link to the patient condition was quite helpful for me. In addition to my core education, I began to "hang out" in the emergency department. As a result, I fell in love with clinical medicine—over research—and I fell in love with all aspects of acute and critical care medicine. This experience has probably driven my career choices more than any other has.

The Urbana program was one year, and I returned to the Chicago campus to do my next three years of medical school. I found myself ahead of my classmates in many of the technical skills because I had done lots of "doctor stuff" in the ER and had seen many clinical situations that my classmates were just now experiencing. On the other hand, I was lost in the bureaucracy of the university and it took some time to adjust. Overall, I found my rotations to be fun, informative and often grueling. I also found myself attracted to the sickest patients as well as the more complicated cases. As I progressed through the various clinical rotations, I moved further and further away from a career in research, although some interest remained.

At the conclusion of my medical training, I considered two specialties: pediatrics and internal medicine. While I had a great interest in emergency medicine one overarching consideration was the fact that I was going into the Army and I needed to factor that into my choice for an initial residency. In the end, I chose internal medicine. When I applied, the Army did not yet have emergency medicine as a choice and I thought adult internal medicine would be my strongest choice.

It turns out that the Army was starting residencies in emergency medicine and, as luck would have it, I started my first year at Brooke Army Medical Center (BAMC) on the same day the Army opened up its first emergency medicine residency there. In addition, my first rotation was in the ER. Like all new trainees, I was assigned a faculty advisor. My advisor was the Army LT. Colonel who developed the Army's approach to emergency medicine and was serving as both the assistant chief of medicine and the consultant to the Army Surgeon General in Emergency Medicine. So right away, I was immersed in the emergency medicine experience.

At the end of my training, I sought fellowship training and considered three subspecialties: critical care, oncology and cardiology. All three had the care of very sick patients as the centerpiece of their work. Unfortunately, I was not accepted into any of the programs and was slotted to be a general internist at Munson Army Hospital at Fort Leavenworth, Kansas. My career took an unexpected turn when several months before I was to leave for duty in Kansas, I received a call from the Army assignments office offering me an opportunity to go to Madigan Army Medical Center as faculty in the emergency medicine residency program that had been started a couple of years earlier. They needed an internist to join their staff and the assignments office was aware of my long-standing interest in emergency medicine. I have always suspected my advisor had some hand in this offer. This is an important point about the importance of mentors in guiding one's career choices and creating opportunities for their mentees. People who were looking out of me have supported me throughout my career. None of us is successful without support from others. This is a guiding life belief and principle for me.

So I went to Tacoma, Washington, and joined an amazing staff tasked with enhancing the teaching program. This assignment offered me several interesting opportunities. First, my hospital commander was very supportive of engagement in professional societies. He called me in shortly after my arrival and offered to support my travel to the National Medical Association's (NMA) conference and to get involved in the Aerospace Military Medicine Section. I did so and became vice chair of the section. Later I became the section chair. This marked my entry into the NMA where I served on several committees, and was one of the founding members of their emergency medicine section.

Second, emergency medicine as a new specialty was an amazing opportunity for significant groundbreaking academic work. I had opportunities to write chapters in all of the major emergency medicine textbooks of the day. The specialty was defining itself separately from other medical disciplines and beginning to write textbooks from the perspective of practitioners in emergency medicine. Frankly, I seized every opportunity that presented itself.

I decided to focus on developing a subspecialty within the field of emergency medicine because of the need to be an expert in something. Two areas of focus presented themselves; emergency medical services and mass casualty disasters including intentional ones like terrorism and weapons of mass destruction including nuclear weapons and bioweapons. I spent a lot of time teaching critical care skills and resuscitation medicine skills like basic life support (BLS), advanced cardiac life support (ACLS), advanced trauma life support (ACLS), pediatric advanced life support (PALS) and advanced trauma life support (ATLS). I took the nuclear weapons hazard course and became knowledgeable about bioweapons. In addition I was assigned as the Chem-Bio expert and medical leader of the Madigan Army Medical Center (MAMC) response team. Because of my internal medicine background, I was also tasked with oversight for the teaching program for nonemergency medicine residents and interns rotating through the urgent and nonurgent side of the emergency department where I developed an expertise in the delivery of acute and urgent ambulatory care.

Like many in Army medicine, health administration is a core part of your duties. I was tasked with being the head of the walk-in clinic for urgent and nonurgent non-appointed visits and appointed visits for the primary care clinic we ran in the ambulatory care portion of the emergency department. I was also tasked with managing the triage program. In this role, I managed a 72,000 annual patient visit ambulatory care clinic that provided care to military members, their families and retirees.

This was a great management and teaching experience. Lots of lessons learned here. Valuing the work of retired physicians that worked in our outpatient clinic was the most important lesson I learned. This outpatient clinic in the emergency department had several retired physicians who were undervalued. We spent my early time there evaluating their work and much to my surprise they were a group of well-trained clinicians who had been relegated to seeing a panel of medically stable military dependents. They were not contributing to the education of the house staff despite a wealth of knowledge. During my tenure, we began to reintegrate them into the teaching program. The life lesson is that there are often great assets in your organization that may be overlooked. Constant evaluation of your organizational assets is essential.

I still had a desire for further subspecialty training because of my interest in critical care medicine. To this end, I applied for and was accepted in a critical care fellowship program at Letterman Army Medical Center in San Francisco, California. Just like two years before, I received a call from the Army assignments office, this time through a call from the head of the assignments division of my former chief of medicine from BAMC and my residency director. The head of medical corps assignments is the physician responsible for career development in the Army. In his wisdom, he shared with me that he had an offer he did not think I could refuse. He requested I come to Washington, DC, to head the emergency department at the Walter Reed Army Medical Center (WRAMC). WRAMC is the Army's flagship academic medical center and this was a big administrative opportunity. It was a tough decision because I wanted to do subspecialty training, but clearly was the next logical step if I wanted an administrative career. This was one of those forks in the road we have during our careers—growth as a subspecialists versus being an administrator—I was being asked to serve as the chief of emergency medicine and the assistant chief of ambulatory care at WRAMC. In addition to my administrative duties as a service chief, I was asked to enhance a teaching program for nonemergency medicine trainees rotating through the emergency department, as I had done at MAMC.

While at Walter Reed, I served as the regional consultant in emergency medicine, taught emergency medicine and internal medicine at the Uniformed Services University of the Health Sciences and served as one of the Army's national faculty for the American Heart Association's ACLS/BLS program. A side duty I had was serving as the Army's representative to the Military Training Network for Resuscitative Medicine (MTN). The MTN was tasked with setting up and providing quality oversight for all of the military's training programs in basic and advanced life support worldwide. My military experience was flush with educational and training opportunities as well as amazing leadership chances and I had lots of mentors and strong command support.

District of Columbia General Hospital— The Private Sector

When I left the Army, I went to become the chairman of the Department of Community Health and Ambulatory Care at DC General Hospital. In this position, I served as the chair of a department in an independent agency of the DC government. We were there as the hospital of last resort to serve the most impoverished residents of the District of Columbia. We were an academic teaching hospital that trained residents from Howard University and Georgetown University. It was a tough environment to work in; chronically underfunded with very sick patients who had few personal resources. The medical staff I worked with was extremely dedicated to the mission and the patients they served. I learned a lot about working to preserve patient dignity here as the core medical community had treated many of these patients as second-class citizens. Some might argue this was my first public health job and others might argue that my time in the military also counts. I actually never saw them that way, but my next job was unquestionably in public health.

District of Columbia Commission of Public Health (CPH)—My First Public Health Job

One afternoon in late December of 1989, my telephone rang on my desk and I found myself talking to then-Washington, D.C., Mayor Marion Barry. The mayor asked me to come see him the next day to discuss a job opportunity. I knew two jobs were on the table but was not sure which one he really wanted me to do. The medical director of the DC ambulance service had been open for some time and I was interested in serving in that role. However, when I met with the mayor, his director of human services and his chief of staff the next morning, I was offered the job as commissioner of public health. This was an enormous opportunity and a big promotion for me. The DC Commission of Public Health is probably the toughest public health job in the country. Poor health statistics, inadequate funding and a complex political environment make it a very difficult job. This job became more difficult when the mayor was arrested on a drug abuse charge within weeks of me being appointed. Because of this challenge, it was clear that the mayor would not run for reelection. That also meant I should not move into the city as planned, which was a requirement for me to be confirmed. I served my tenure as acting commissioner. This made my tenure as commissioner more difficult as many people felt I was going to continue to be in an acting position pending the results of the next election. Sharon Pratt Kelly was the surprise winner of the 1990 election and was sworn in as the first female African American mayor of a major city in January 1991. I had the privilege of serving for about 10 months of her tenure after which she appointed her own health commissioner, my friend and colleague Dr. Mohammad Akhter. During this period, we launched an aggressive effort to address the city's growing HIV/AIDS epidemic, which was shifting to the African American community and beginning to show up in women. We also saw the first significant drop in the city's infant mortality rate and improvements in the immunization rate.

Health Policy Consultant and Emergency Physician

I left the DC government in November 1991 and returned to the practice of emergency medicine. For the next two-and-a-half years, I worked as an emergency physician in a busy suburban hospital. I also focused a lot of my other efforts in health policy around issues of emergency medicine, disasters and terrorism. One evening my telephone rang and the DC mayor's chief of staff was on the telephone. I was asked to return to DC government, this time as the medical director of the ambulance service. This position, which made me a deputy fire chief, did not require confirmation or a move into the city. The mayor was running for reelection and the current EMS medical director was leaving for a position in Maryland and the mayor wanted to ensure a smooth transition into the position. There had been significant improvements in the functioning of the ambulance service and the mayor clearly wanted to both sustain these gains and continue with improvements of the system. I was a logical choice as I had recruited the previous director as one of my last acts as health commissioner and I, of course, knew the system well. I was not sure about my career goals at that time and the mayor was in the middle of her reelection quest, so I negotiated to come on board as the interim director pending a national search for a replacement.

DC Emergency Ambulance Bureau

I spent 10 months as the interim director, during which I was credited with continuing improvements in the quality of care provided and shortening response times. I also began a process to rebuild the ambulance fleet. The mayor lost her reelection bid to Marion Barry who had made a remarkable political comeback after his drug conviction. As for me, I decided that it was time to return to public health and begin a career, in earnest, in health policy.

Maryland Department of Health and Mental Hygiene (DHMH)

Dr. Martin Wasserman, who had been the Montgomery County, Maryland, health officer when I was the D.C. commissioner of public health, now served as the secretary of health for Maryland in the newly elected administration of Governor Parris Glendening. Marty invited me to consider being his deputy of public health services. Marty and I had worked together when I was the DC health commissioner and he was the Montgomery County health commissioner. Montgomery County is a Maryland county adjacent to Washington, DC. I was honored to apply and was appointed as one of three deputy secretaries. The other two were for the state Medicaid program and departmental operations. In many ways, this was a big decision because it was a tremendous cut in pay and meant I could no longer practice clinical medicine. The department is a major regulatory agency and the lawyers felt a clinical practice would be a conflict of interest for me. Let me say this was not only the most important career decision in my life but also one that totally changed the direction of my life's work. Fortunately, for me, it turned out to be the most rewarding position I have ever had, recognizing the amazing experience I am still having at the American Public Health Association.

I served a total of eight years in the Department of Health and Mental Hygiene (DHMH). As deputy for public health, I oversaw the traditional public health areas of infectious disease control, maternal child health, the state public health laboratory and local public health. In addition, the medical examiner, developmental disabilities, substance abuse and mental health were programs all under my charge.

After four years as deputy, I was promoted to be the secretary in early spring 1999 and was now responsible for the state regulatory agencies, departmental operations and the state Medicaid program. During this period, we were successful in substantially improving the health of Marylanders. This was a team effort and in many ways the result of my having built a solid well-functioning team during my tenure. Of note, I was the first African American health secretary in the state's history. I also had the opportunity to serve nationally as the president of the Association of State and Territorial Health Officials (ASTHO) at a time of national crisis; the terrorist attack on September 11, 2001, and discovery of the anthrax letters one month later.

During my tenure in Maryland, we handled many other public health emergencies to include a statewide drought, a tornado in southern Maryland, a 700-person foodborne outbreak in St. Mary's County, and an outbreak of a newly discovered red tide like organism called Pfisteria in the rivers of Maryland's Eastern Shore. The breadth of my experiences in Maryland provided a wealth of leadership lessons for me.

American Public Health Association (APHA)

At the end of the Glendening administration, I came to the American Public Health Association (APHA) as the executive director where I have served since December 2002 and am now the association's second longest serving executive director. APHA is the nation's oldest association of public health and reflects the history of public health in the United States. APHA is a complex membership association with over 50,000 members and a long, proud history both domestically and internationally. I have had the privilege of leading a strong team of talented individuals working to ensure the right to health and health care; building the public health infrastructure; and working to achieve health equity for all. Providing national leadership as the head of this important organization poses numerous leadership challenges and opportunities. My life experiences have prepared me well to address the many leadership challenges that present themselves daily on the national level. Having to address actions of national political leaders, public and private organizations as well as public expectations to improve the public health makes this a challenging and rewarding position. I have found that there are five core leadership lessons.

My Six Core Leadership Lessons

In my experience, there are six leadership lessons that I have learned during my life.

1. Work and play well with others and treat everyone with respect. When in conflict over the right thing to do, always do what is in the best interest of the people you are trying to lead.

2. Know where you want to go and stay focused on it. Steer your organization and its members to get there but do not do the rowing. Steering lets you keep a focus on the big picture while letting your team figure out how to get you there. It empowers your staff and helps them build ownership in the final product.
3. Understand how things work in the organization you are working for and its culture. You cannot influence an organization's direction until you understand the organization. I am not a fan of cleaning house and changing direction 180 degrees. You may need to do that at some point but usually this delays organizational progress. I prefer to spend the time developing the case for change and building the leadership loyalty to get us there.
4. All things have a political element to them and politics is not a dirty word. Sincerity is what's important. This means that sometimes you have to take an indirect route to achieve your goal; or play chess not checkers. Not everyone is going to be a supporter and there are people out there who, for a variety of reasons, are out to see that you don't succeed. To manage these sharks I follow a set of principles that are attributed to the French philosopher Voltaire. This treatise, entitled "How to Swim with Sharks", is a useful guide for those of us in leadership positions. It recommends that we learn to first be good swimmers and then how to manage in shark-filled waters (Cousteau, 1812, 1987). I strongly recommend this guide to all who find themselves in a leadership position.
5. Be the best in your field that you can be. I am a physician first and an administrator second. My approach to my oath as a physician informs all of my decisions. Be the best in your field; your stature in your field is an important asset to being a leader. People follow people they can respect for their core expertise. You still must be a good manager and leader, but no one follows a "leader" they can't professionally respect.
6. No one got to where they are without help from others. No one!

Reference

Cousteau, V. (1812, 1987). How to swim with sharks: A primer. *Perspectives in Biology and Medicine, 30*(4),486–489.

CHAPTER FOUR

Footsteps of My Father

JOHN R. LUMPKIN, MD, MPH, FACEP, FACME, FAAN

"Change will not come if we wait for some other person or some other time. We are the ones we've been waiting for. We are the change we seek."
—President Barak Obama

I count myself very fortunate to have had an opportunity to positively impact the world around me. Combining personal interests, intellectual curiosity and a sense of purpose that my life's work be directed towards values of social justice and fairness guided my career choices. I am a product of my upbringing and the experiences derived from the times of my youth. With a career rooted in both intellectual curiosity and my most deeply held values a high degree of commitment came naturally. To paraphrase Lord Chesterfield, "If it is worth doing it is worth doing well".

When you follow in the path of your father, you learn to walk like him.—Ashanti Proverb

Both my mother and father committed themselves to labor union and community organizing in order to achieve improvements in safety, equity and quality of life.

My father, Frank Lumpkin was born in 1916, the third child in a family of 10 children in Washington, Georgia. The grandson of a slave he experienced brutal Jim Crow conditions during his early years. During the Depression Frank worked the Florida orange groves with his supervisors carrying guns to remind the workers not break the branches. He picked cotton in Louisiana, worked as a chauffeur in Atlanta and was a professional boxer in Orlando, Florida. Frank moved with his family to Buffalo, New York during the 1940s as part of the great northern migration. He worked as a mechanic on Liberty ships during World War II and thereafter worked in steel mills in Buffalo and later in Chicago, Illinois. Despite his eighth grade education Frank was widely read and placed a high value on education (The History Makers, 2018).

My mother, Beatrice Shapiro Lumpkin was third of four children of Russian Jewish immigrants who fled the pogroms of 1903. Her father escaped from a Tsarist prison with the aid of his soon to be wife prior to immigrating to New York where he worked as a tailor and she did laundry. Grandma Rodhe also worked at the Triangle Shirtwaist Factory. A frequently recounted family story described her good fate at having been home on maternity leave during the fire in a workplace with no emergency exits that resulted in the deaths of 146 of her coworkers (Wikipedia, n.d(e)). My mother graduated from Hunter College for Women with a degree in education. She completed a master's degree in mathematics later in life. Mom worked as a laborer in the laundry industry, trained technicians to use radar during World War II, was a chemist in the steel industry, a writer in the electronics industry and finally worked as a teacher. She researched multicultural influences in the development of mathematics and published the first article demonstrating that the ancient Egyptians had and used the concept of zero. Beatrice went on to develop and publish multicultural approaches to teaching elementary mathematics and science.

In 1951 my parents lived on the Near-Southside of Chicago. The closest hospital was Michael Reese known to provide excellent maternity care that was unavailable to the poor. As my family did not have much money my mother timed her arrival at the hospital, in labor, so that I would be born at Michael Reese Hospital. I am the youngest of four children. In 1954 our family moved to Gary, Indiana to be closer to my mother's work at US Steel.

These formative childhood years unfolded against the backdrop of profound social upheaval and struggle in the United States. Another family story recounts the events following the brutal murder of Emmett Till while visiting Mississippi and the return to Chicago of his mutilated body (Wikipedia, n.d.(a)). My father's sister Jonnie Ellis was one of a group of civil rights activists that helped convince Emmett Till's mother to have an open casket funeral. This act led to widely publicized revelations about the brutality of his murder and helped to ignite the civil rights movement. My parents were active in the civil rights movement and in local politics. I recall my father's election as the Democratic precinct committeeman for our area in Gary, Indiana. He organized community members and opened the Wooded Highlands Democratic Club as a place where they could gather. As a young child I often joined him at these gatherings where they discussed the events of the day. Later in life my father led the workers of Wisconsin Steel Works as they demanded fair treatment when International Harvester closed the mill in a manner that resulted in lost pensions for thousands of long-term steelworkers. His efforts led to a $14 million dollar settlement for the former workers and a return of his pension. Under Frank Lumpkin's leadership, the Wisconsin Steel Save Our Jobs Committee provided social services, a political voice and ultimately payment of pension funds for the *disposed* steelworkers for many years (The History Makers, 2018).

In 1961 we moved to Broadview, Illinois a suburb west of Chicago to be closer to mother's new job writing manuals for electronics kits being developed and sold by Knight Electronics, a precursor to what is now known as RadioShack. To test out the clarity of the directions in the manuals my siblings and I were challenged to follow them and build the devices. Exposure to my older siblings who excelled in math and science and experiences with electronics and chemistry fostered and fueled my scientific curiosity. I was fortunate to have had the encouragement of public school teachers who recognized and nurtured my interest in science. After school my friends and I would experiment with electronics, physics and chemistry. At Proviso East High School I took every math and science course that was offered.

In the summer of 1967, I attended a summer National Science Foundation enrichment program at Carnegie Tech., now Carnegie Mellow University working in a microbiology laboratory and learning computer programming. At age 16 I decided that my future lay in a new field, biophysics, which would encompass my many scientific interests. With strong test scores I was recruited to the Massachusetts Institute of Technology in the fall of 1969.

All things being equal, I would have charged into a career in hard science, but all things were not equal.

The earliest settlers in the area that became Broadview were African American. That originally settled area of Broadview was racially diverse when I grew up there. My home life instilled in me the rightness of treating others fairly regardless of their ethnicity, socioeconomic status or race and my classmates and schoolyard friends came from diverse backgrounds. The remainder of the town of Broadview outside of the older portion, however, was exclusively White. Traveling north of Roosevelt Road was traveling into a different world altogether where I learned to endure racial epithets freely spouted. All of this growing awareness of self occurred within the backdrop of the civil rights and anti-Vietnam War movements. I watched with horror the attacks on the marchers in Selma, Alabama and with pride Martin Luther King's March on Washington. I remember vividly hearing the news of John F. Kennedy's, Martin Luther King's and Malcolm X's assassinations. In 1966 I marched with my family and Martin Luther King, Jr. in Chicago and in 1967 we traveled to Washington to protest against the Vietnam War. It was through civil rights activities in Broadview and neighboring Maywood, Illinois that I met Fred Hampton, then young civil rights leader who would later become the head of the Black Panther Party in Chicago.

Growing up, I had a multitude of role models from the struggle for civil rights, worker's rights, equity and peace. These youthful experiences became an important part of my moral compass serving as the foundation for my subsequent work and the basis of my approach to leadership. In high school I participated in the typical activities including science club, chess club and the track team competing in the 440 yard run and pole vaulting. Yet, in an environment of racial unrest, political activity was also on my agenda. I formed the Students for a Better Proviso that pressed the school administration for fairness and justice for student of all races.

Don't set sail on someone else's star.—African Proverb

During my freshman year at MIT conflicting directions in my life reached an inflection point. It was 1969 and the entire nation was in turmoil or at least it seemed to be from my perspective. In December, police from the Cook County States Attorney's office gunned down Fred Hampton and Mark Clark in their sleep and the Vietnam War was raging (Wikipedia, n.d.(b)). I was active in the Boston civil rights and peace movements when I realized that continuing on a career path focused on hard science would end up a life in the laboratory. While that was intellectually attractive, my obligation to be of service to others drew me in a different direction. Pursuing a career in medicine allowed me to be of service to humanity while continuing my fascination with science. I returned to my hometown of Chicago to attend the Honors Medical Program at Northwestern University. Continuing to balance study with local political activity I was also privileged to work with Dr. Quinton Young's Medical Committee for Human Rights (Wikipedia, n.d.(c)).

Medical school was challenging and intellectually engaging. Vera Markovin, MD and her husband Leo King were long time close family friends. Dr. Markovin was an early practitioner of Emergency Medicine. On Christmas Eve my freshman year of medical school, I shadowed Dr. Markovin as she worked in the emergency department of Oak Park hospital. In 1971, the specialty of Emergency Medicine was in its infancy. The American College of Emergency Physicians was three years old and the first residents in Emergency Medicine were still in training. That evening, shadowing Vera Markovin I was hooked. The pace, the challenge of seeing one unknown patient after another and the diversity of problems matched my broad range of interests. After the holidays, I returned to school determined to figure out how to become an emergency physician. In discussion with my advisor, we plotted out a course of study that used my electives to build upon the foundational required medical school coursework. The first senior year elective was a rotation at the University of Chicago emergency medicine department, site of the third established emergency medicine residency program in the United States. This elective was followed by rotations in occupational medicine and physical and rehabilitation medicine.

After completing a rotating internship in anesthesia, I entered the University of Chicago residency in Emergency Medicine in 1976, headed by Peter Rosen, MD, one of the grandfathers of the new specialty (Emergency Medicine Residents' Association, n.d.). To my knowledge I was the first African American resident in Emergency Medicine in the United States. During my residency, Dr. Frank Baker led the development of the Chicago Emergency Medical Services (EMS) System with the University of Chicago being one of three managing Resource Hospitals for the city. Residents were encouraged to teach paramedics and were required to provide pre-hospital medical control via the radio system. Through active engagement in system operations, I gained an understanding of the function of the EMS system, the role and capabilities of the pre-hospital provider system and the science behind pre-hospital care.

During residency, I remained engaged in Chicago's South Shore community where I lived. This was community of fine old homes vacated by "white flight", the out-migration of well-to-do Whites whose ownership was replaced by middle-class African Americans. In 1977, I headed up the 7th Ward campaign for Harold Washington as he made his first, unsuccessful run for Mayor of Chicago (Wikipedia, n.d.(c)). It was a great learning process with our team successfully delivering one of the five wards out of fifty that Harold Washington won. After the election my community engagement continued as President of the Bryn Mawr East Area Council of the South Shore Commission, a collection of block clubs engaged in community redevelopment and activism with a social justice agenda. Balancing political activism with residency training was challenging and valuable. It provided a well-rounded lifestyle and sense of self, grounded in the day-to-day concerns of people in my community.

After completing residency, I was invited to join the faculty of the Department of Emergency Medicine at the University of Chicago becoming a Co-Medical Director of the Chicago South EMS System. I became involved in organized Emergency Medicine through the Illinois College of Emergency Physicians (ICEP) through which I was introduced more fully to the role of state government. Having a history of community engagement and political experience that most of my emergency medicine colleagues lacked, I was appointed to chair the Socio-Economic Committee of ICEP and to take the lead in negotiating the first EMS Act for the State of Illinois. As the lead negotiator, I worked with Dr. Bernard Turnock, Chief of EMS for the Illinois Department of Public Health (IDPH), Representative James Reilly, the bill sponsor and the Illinois State Medical Society as the bill went through revisions and was finally adopted. Negotiating this bill through the legislature, working with lobbyists, IDPH and the Governor's office I gained firsthand knowledge and experience that would serve me well throughout my career. In 1981, after the Emergency Medical Services Systems Act was enacted I was appointed to chair the Illinois EMS Advisory Committee by Governor James Thompson. This opportunity had me digging deeper into the regulatory process as we grappled with revising the state paramedic and emergency medical technician examination and defining the role of hospitals, physicians, EMTs, fire departments and all of the other stakeholders in the system. It also set me up for my first experience being "fired" from a job with a resultant major transition in my career.

You always learn a lot more when you lose than when you win.—African Proverb

In 1983 Harold Washington was elected the first African American mayor of Chicago. I worked in his first unsuccessful campaign in 1977 and again in for his election in 1983. After the election, Dr. Quinton Young headed up Mayor Washington's health transition team. Dr. Young asked me to write a transition paper about EMS services in Chicago. Drawing upon my experience in the EMS system in Illinois and a site-visit to New York City, I wrote a paper recommending that the EMS service be pulled out of the Chicago Fire Department and made into a separate service. As I learned later, most transition reports sit on the shelf having been read by only a few people. One person who did read my report was the new Commissioner of the Chicago Fire Department. Taking my recommendations as a personal affront, he looked for ways to retaliate against the University of Chicago Hospitals and Clinic system threatening their status managing the EMS system on the Southside of Chicago. Responding to this pressure, the department chairman suggested that it was time for me to move on.

This event occurred at a pivotal point in my career. I was 32 years old, and recently elected Vice-Speaker of the American College of Emergency Physicians

(ACEP). Over the last year I had been recruited for chairmanship positions in Emergency Medicine in other cities. At the same time, I had increasing frustrations as too often people presented in preventable, dire conditions due to lack of access to health care or pharmaceuticals. Others had their health impacted by addictions, violence, poverty and preventable injuries. Prior exposure to health policymaking at the state level and the national level through ACEP led me to consider another career pathway. Using the imposed transition as an opportunity, I enrolled in a master's degree program in health policy and resources at the University of Illinois School of Public Health. Attending school while working in a community emergency department, I began to see other ways to improve health through prevention and public policy first in the field of injury prevention and later through population health approaches.

The care of human life and happiness, and not their destruction, is the first and only object of good government.—Thomas Jefferson

My first and biggest challenge as Associate Director was reforming the regulation of nursing homes. Nursing home advocates were decrying the level of care and ineffectiveness of regulation by IDPH. Nursing home owners complained that regulation focused on the wrong things and were applied inconsistently. Allegations of favoritism towards some nursing homes were complaints shared by both advocates and owners. During meetings of senior staff and frontline inspectors, I was heartened to find so many people who gave lie to the stereotypes of public workers being uncaring and lazy. IDPH health regulation staff wanted to do the right thing and was looking to leadership to help them do just that. Working together we developed a mission statement, "Firm, Fair and Consistent" and proceeded to make that the operating principle for staff at all levels. Early in my tenure, I received many calls from "connected" individuals asking for special treatment. One prominent nursing home owner called me and said, "My nursing home was given an 'A' violation, we will take a 'B.' 'A' level violations carried a $10,000 fine and a requirement for an immediate plan of correction." This case involved a feeding tube being placed in the resident's lung instead of the stomach resulting in the resident's death. Having reviewed the case personally, I told the nursing home owner that we were going to stick with the "A" level violation. I had been empowered by Dr. Turnock and the Governor's office to deny those requests by sticking to our "Firm, Fair and Consistent" approach. Later, I received a call from the same nursing home owner who said, "The word on the street is that you cannot be reached." I responded that I made sure to return all of my calls in a timely fashion. He responded, "That is not what I mean." As his meaning sunk in, I thanked him for the compliment because that was exactly the message I wanted to send. Fines were assessed and our rate of enforcement rose to meet national standards. We published reports of findings and sanctions to enable the public to make more informed decisions about care of their loved ones. A year later our approach was challenged in a meeting with a group of predominantly Jewish nursing home owners led by former State Legislator Pete Peters. They showed me an inspection report that cited a facility for having unpalatable food solely because it was Kosher. This was a statement that could only be based in anti-Semitism or ignorance. I was stunned and immediately withdrew that violation. This occurrence underscored for me the importance of cultural competency for fairness in government regulation and policy development.

In August, 1990, towards the end of the administration of Governor Thompson, Dr. Turnock resigned his position to join the faculty of the University of Illinois Chicago. I was invited to meet with Governor Thompson and was offered the position of Director of the Illinois Department of Public Health. I responded that I was honored and interested. In a moment of foresight driven by a desire to delay the pay cut associated with moving from a civil-service to a political appointment position, I requested that my appointment be acting. That decision turned out to have a huge impact on my tenure at IDPH. This was in the middle of a heated gubernatorial election campaign between Attorney General Neil Hartigan (Democrat) and Secretary of State Jim Edgar (Republican). After 14 years of Republican Gubernatorial Leadership under Jim Thompson the public mood was for change. Jim Edgar's campaign realized that positioning the candidate as separate from the prior governor was important for success. Weeks after I was named Acting Director political reporter Dick Kay, in the final debate, asked candidate Jim Edgar if he was going to keep any of Governor Thompson's agency directors. The answer was a clear and unqualified, "No." I realized that as an "acting director" I was one of only three directors not covered by that edict.

However, the transition from one administration to another, even of the same political party, is always a time of uncertainty in administrative agencies and was especially so for me. I had been active in Democratic Party campaigns in support of Harold Washington and Carol Moseley Braun, among others, and had ongoing working relationships with both of these local leaders. However, I had also built up relationships with key leaders in Illinois public health and members of both political parties. My interview with Governor-elect Jim Edgar was an interesting experience. I made clear that I was a registered Democrat and had been active in the anti-Vietnam War and Civil Rights movements. He was accepting of my activist history and felt that we could work together. It was clear to me that this was a man whom I could respect. My instincts were on target as he became one of the most respected Governors of the State in recent memory. At the same time, Mayor Richard M. Dailey was looking for a Chicago Commissioner of Health and I was honored to have been offered that position. While it would have been more comfortable working in a Democratic administration closer to home, the broader scope and opportunity for greater societal impact led me to take the State position. It was a major turning point in my career that brought challenge and an opportunity to make a difference. Once part of the Governor's cabinet, I found that political differences were less important than keeping the focus on protecting the health of the people of the State which the Governor's office wholeheartedly supported.

One of my first accomplishments addressed the significant racial and ethnic health disparities in health. Measures of health determinants and outcomes demonstrated that minority and poor communities were not seeing the same health gains as the White and wealthier populations. I felt it was important for the Illinois Department of Public Health to address these problems and formed the first Office of Minority Health Affairs in Illinois State Government. Learning from my earlier experience with the Jewish nursing home owners, I realized that establishing the office and using an *equity-based approach* to policy at the top would not be successful if our staff did not better understand the people and problems they were working to help improve. In 1992 we became the first state public health agency in the nation to require that all staff complete a cultural competency course.

Throughout my tenure at IDPH, I believed that it was important to track national developments and participate in national organizations. That enabled me to gain new experiences and insights into novel ways to improve public health in the state. For example, my interest in injury prevention developed while I was a student at the University of Illinois School of Public Health. Pursuing that at the state level led to invitations to serve on advisory boards for the Center for Injury Prevention at Centers for Disease Control and Prevention (CDC). In that capacity, I reviewed national best practice and brought new ideas back to Illinois. While at the University of Chicago, one of my tasks as Chicago South Co-Project Medical Director was disaster preparedness. We worked with the Chicago Fire Department, other pre hospital providers, the Metropolitan Chicago Hospital Council, the Chicago Police Department, emergency management agencies and others to plan responses for mass casualty events due to transportation crashes or explosions in public venues. I brought that interest with me and, with time, IDPH was in the forefront of biological agent preparedness with a program first implemented in 1995. Leslee Stein-Spencer RN, IDPH Chief of Emergency Services System, led the development of a disaster response system as an overlay over the EMS and trauma center systems drawing on resources tested and refined in everyday care. Modernizing the state public health laboratory was of critical importance and a high priority. While the lab was an effective and efficient service, it was deficient in what is now considered a key foundational service, molecular biology. I had submitted requests to fund laboratory expansion to the Bureau of the Budget for a number of years without success. I was finally successful in getting funding after an outbreak of necrotizing fasciitis in a few nursing homes in Decatur, Illinois. "Necrotizing fasciitis is a serious bacterial skin infection that spreads quickly and kills … soft tissue. … [and] can become life threatening in a very short amount of time" (Centers for Disease Control and Prevention, 2017, para. 1). Noting that our response would have been improved with an enhanced laboratory finally convinced the Governor's office to support my request. The molecular biology capability gained was immediately useful in explaining the epidemiology of major outbreaks in the following years. It was also important for testing white powders submitted by a frightened public after the Anthrax attacks following September 11th, 2001 as well as in testing for the emerging West Nile Virus outbreak in 2002.

My early interest in technology led me to purchase one of the early IBM personal computers in 1983. I rapidly grasped the role that computers and information systems could play in improving the effectiveness and efficiency of public health and health care service delivery. Database management coursework while a student at the University of Illinois School of Public Health prepared me to introduce enhanced information technology to IDPH. I led the redesign of the long-term care information system and the adoption of agency-wide email services. In 1993, Deputy Director Jim Nelson and I implemented the first integrated, paperless maternal/child health information system in the nation, Cornerstone. The program was designed to meet the needs of frontline staff while minimizing paper documentation required for administrative purposes. In over three hundred sites across the state, public health nurses, case managers and public clinics used the information system to integrate the Special Supplemental Nutrition Program for Women, Infant, and Children (WIC), well child visits, immunizations and lead poisoning treatment services. I always felt it was important for senior leaders to understand the realities of program implementation on the front lines. I regularly visited local health departments to gain insight into the day-to-day operation of the public health system. On one visit in Southern Illinois, I was able to see the fruits of our labors when a local health department case manager interviewed a client, referred her to a well child clinic and printed up her WIC coupons using the new system. I felt especially proud when she finished with the young women and looked up and said, "I am done." Because the system was paperless, she had no time sheets or administrative forms to fill out. That sense of accomplishment was quickly tempered when I went down the hall and saw another staff member with three computers on her desk each linked into a different state government information system. Elsewhere, I saw staff at a large clinical laboratory in the Chicago area taking information from a computer printout to fill out public health infectious disease reports by hand. I knew full well that back at the health department, other staff were taking those written reports and entering them in the state infectious disease system.

Again, the search for solutions required looking outside Illinois. Public health information systems suffered from the same obstacle that plagued health care information systems, the lack of standards to enable inoperability. The flow of data requires trust between the exchanging partners and standards to assure that the data can be used without the loss of meaning. A business, a community or a state could not set these standards. They had to be set at the national level. As a member of the Association of State and Territorial Health Officials (ASTHO), I had access to senior officials of the US Department of Health and Human Services and the Centers for Disease Control and Prevention (CDC). Representing ASTHO, I was able to successfully argue that funding silos at the federal level was part of the problem. With agreement from Phil Lee, MD, Assistant Secretary of Health of the Department of Health and Human Services (DHHS), categorical funds from the Health Resources and Services Administration's Maternal and Child Health Block Grant and the Centers for Disease Control and Prevention's immunization programs could be used by states to develop integrated information systems along the lines of the Illinois Cornerstone maternal and child health information system. As a result of these activities, I was appointed to chair the National Committee on Vital and Health Statistics (NCVHS) immediately after the adoption of the Health Insurance Portability and Accountability Act (HIPAA). Working on federal advisory boards was as much education as service. Members of the NCVHS included some of the brightest minds in the nation on issues of data standards, privacy and public health surveillance. Equally as talented was the committee staff drawn from many of the United States Department of Health and Human Services (USDHHS) agencies and operating divisions. While the committee initially focused on the privacy, security and transaction standards mandated by HIPAA, we also were able to develop a national vision for a broad approach to using data and information systems to transform health and health care. This vision was published as Information for Health, a Strategy for Building the National Health Information Infrastructure (Lumpkin, 2001). The report included recommendations for the appointment of a National Coordinator for Health Information Technology, building out the personal health information dimension and enhancing interoperability to allow the free flow of information so that people could have the right information at right time to make health and health care decisions.

In 1998, Jim Edgar left office and George Ryan was elected Governor. After the election, I reached out to his staff and the members of the transition committee expressing my interest in staying on as Director of IDPH. One of the new Governor's closest advisors was Pete Peters, the head of the predominantly Jewish nursing home association with whom I had worked years earlier. Although we were on opposite sides on many issues related to nursing homes enforcement, we had developed a mutual respect based on fair and consistent implementation of the State rules and regulations. Based on his advice and that of other supporters, I was reappointed. This was the second time in my career where adversaries who were treated with respect and fairness positively influenced my career, demonstrating that in a civil society disagreement need not lead to unpleasantness and conflict. The Ryan administration was a time of very high highs and very low lows. Governor Ryan was the first sitting Governor to visit Cuba in 1999. I was designated to head up the health portion of that delegation on the US State Department sanctioned trip. We toured hospitals, clinics, medical schools and a pharmaceutical plant. Everywhere we went we were treated warmly and with respect. The highlight of the visit was meeting with the Governor, Illinois Legislative leaders, cabinet officers and Cuban President Fidel Castro. During the seven hour meeting and dinner, the conversation ranged from health issues and agriculture practices to religion and education. A year later, I accompanied Governor Ryan as part of a delegation to open a State of Illinois trade office in South Africa. The health leaders in the delegation toured the Chris Hani Baragwanath Hospital in Soweto. We were all impressed to see the largest hospital in Africa and the third largest in the world in the middle of one of the poorest ghettos in Johannesburg. Another highlight of that trip was visiting the former home of Nelson Mandela and the infamous Robbins Island Prison. These trips were followed by other important policy initiatives including George Ryan's moratorium on implementing the death penalty. And then the wheels of the Governor's administration fell off. Allegations related to corruption began cropping up and rumors of a federal investigation began to circulate. The Ryan administration went from sweeping policy initiatives to a bunker mentality.

Despite the challenges facing the governor, progress continued within IDPH. With funds from the tobacco settlement, we were able to implement a groundbreaking approach to prohibit youth tobacco use. With millions of dollars flowing into the State, we were forced to compete with other State priorities for the new funds. One of the biggest obstacles was the belief that public health could not do anything about teen smoking. With an initial allocation of $5 million dollars we set out to prove that public health programs could make a difference. One of my favorite parables is about peanut butter and bread. If you try to spread a fixed amount of peanut butter over a number of loaves of bread, at some point you become unable to taste the peanut butter. Faced with the choice of spreading $5 million dollars over 96 local health departments, I choose to concentrate the funds in one community to demonstrate effectiveness with the hope and expectation that success there would lead to a larger portion of the tobacco settlement funding later on. Thus began a program called IDecide focused on Rockford in Winnebago County, population 300,000. It was large enough to demonstrate effect and small enough that a campaign based in youth empowerment combined with media messaging could be implemented. The program was an immediate success with the Youth Behavioral Risk Factor Survey demonstrating an 11% reduction in smoking during the first year. Advertisements were co-developed with a teen leadership board based on a mythical All Smoke High (ASH) School where students were required to smoke. The TV advertisements received wide attention in the community and were awarded a Silver Anvil by the Public Relations Society of America. Building on this success, the budget was increased to $10 Million and the program expanded to seven counties in Central Illinois. In early negotiations with the Bureau of the Budget, an initial commitment was made to add $15 million to the program to launch it in the Chicago Metropolitan Area the following year. Then IDecide became a casualty of political machinations. The Governor's office was approached by the Speaker of the House to allocate $10 Million for a billboard campaign against tobacco in the Chicago area. Relying on clear evidence that billboards were ineffective in the absence of a comprehensive approach similar to the one we had implemented in Rockford, I advised against funding that request. At the same time local health departments in the Chicago area met with the Speaker of the House complaining that none of the public health tobacco funds were being used in Chicago. The following budget year, the House Speaker zeroed out all funding for youth tobacco interdiction. Once again the greater power of politics over science was demonstrated.

At 8:00 a.m. on September 11, 2001, I was driving to the University of Illinois School of Public Health for our first major conference on oral health. I tuned to the news radio station and listened to reports of an aircraft flying into the side of the World Trade Center. As I neared the school a second plane rammed into the second tower and both were aflame. A television in the lobby displayed the raging infernos and then the first building collapsed. Like everyone else in this nation, my life was irrevocably changed. All state buildings were closed and following our emergency response plan, I spent the day in the City of Chicago Emergency Operations Center (EOC). It was an eerie feeling to sit at my station coordinating with the Illinois State Emergency Operation Center while the collapse of the twin towers played and replayed on the large video monitors. It became even more surreal as I looked out of the window at the Sears Tower, now the Willis Tower, which had just become the tallest building in the United States wondering if it too was going to be targeted. The next day, I drove to the IDPH central office in Springfield Illinois as the state reviewed and revised our plan. I was placed on the Public Safety Subcabinet with the State Police, Fire Marshall and the National Guard as they discussed the merits of arming the State Troopers protecting the nuclear power plants with automatic weapons. As time passed, and no new attacks occurred, a new normal began to set in until October 5th when the first victim of the Anthrax attacks died. That was when the full scope of our careful preparedness and planning came together. With an upgraded public health laboratory with molecular biology capacity we were one of the few states that could perform our own Anthrax testing. Long-standing relationships with the Illinois State Police, Illinois Emergency Management Agency and the Federal Bureau of Investigation facilitated the response to citizen reports of suspicious "white powder." We were fortunate that no incidents occurred in the state but the experience cemented a stronger working relationship with law enforcement and the emergency response system. Afterwards the Director of the Illinois Emergency Management Agency would regularly state, "Every disaster has a public health component."

George Ryan became a one-term governor when he announced he was not going to run for re-election. In November 2002 Rod Blagojevich became the first Democratic Governor of Illinois in 26 years. It was time for another transition. Despite working for three Republican Governors, the fact that I was openly a Democratic led me to be optimistic about my chances of staying on as Director of IDPH. Even after 12 years, there were still many things to be done to continue to rebuild a department impacted by decades of de-professionalization. In the 1950s a physician, nurse or other health professional headed almost every division at IDPH. By 1990, there were only four physicians in the agency. During my tenure, I paid special attention to hiring professionals, bringing in physicians, a PhD epidemiologist and a veterinarian among others. All Division Chiefs were trained at the Motorola Institute in Six-Sigma quality improvement to incorporate a continuous quality management mindset into the agency's culture. I relished the possibility of working with a new administration to continue the process of rebuilding the agency and public health in the state. This was not to be. All of my contacts with the Governor's transition team returned with the answer that they were looking to go in a different direction. A family friend was informed by a close confidant of the Governor-elect, that I was "too straight" for them. Despite the fact that I felt sorrow in leaving the agency, in retrospect I am proud that my attempts to be a professional who was Fair, Firm and Consistent in promoting public health was not compatible with the Rod Blagojevich administration.

The long and short of it was that I was again at an inflection point in my career. My work on health information policy had opened a number of opportunities. I had worked with US Department of Health and Human Services (HHS) Secretary Tommy Thompson as he became an advocate for the role of health information technology in transforming health care. He was encouraging me to accept a position as HHS Assistant Secretary of Health. At the same time, a recruiter for the Robert Wood Johnson Foundation (RWJF), an organization that I had respected for years, had approached me. As part of the interview process, I met the incoming President and CEO, Dr. Risa Lavizzo-Mourey. I was attracted by the ability of philanthropy to make real changes in the health of the country without the constraints of politics and administrative bureaucracy. While trying to decide between the two positions, the World Health Organization (WHO) was considering the world's first public health treaty, the WHO Framework Convention on Tobacco Control. The Assistant Secretary for Health frequently served as the US representative to the WHO and the Bush Administration choose not to ratify the treaty. I did not think that I could be the spokesperson who would have to justify that policy to the rest of the world. Deciding to work where I had the greatest opportunity to have impact and improve health make the choice to go to the Robert Wood Johnson Foundation (RWJF), an easy choice.

It was with a sense of excitement regarding the ability to make a difference on the national stage that I joined RWJF as Senior Vice President and Director of the Health Care Group, a role that brought me full circle. I was challenged to bring my experience in public health systems and practice and apply it to improve the quality, effectiveness and efficiency of the health care system more broadly. I was able to draw on past experiences in new ways.

It was the movement to RWJF that gave me the opportunity to participate in the birth of another medical specialty, Medical Informatics. Two years after arriving at the Foundation, I found myself in conversation with Don Detmer, MD, a leading visionary on health information systems and then the Executive Director of the American Medical Informatics Association (AMIA) (Wikipedia, n.d.(d)). We lamented that hospitals and health systems had no way to determine if the physicians that were selected to lead the implementation of their electronic health systems were qualified. In fact we had heard stories about physicians being selected to head up adoption of an electronic medical record system with the sole qualification being having a home computer. Drawing on my knowledge and experience during the development of Emergency Medicine we proceeded to chart out a path for a medical sub-specialty in Clinical Informatics. Our first step was to reach out to two of my emergency medicine contacts. The first was my former University of Chicago emergency medicine resident Louis Ling, MD who was President of the American Board of Emergency Medicine. Dr. Ling sponsored a preliminary meeting with other medical specialty boards about the feasibility and desirability of starting a sub-specialty board in clinical informatics. Subsequently, the American Board of Preventive Medicine agreed to host the sub-specialty board and make it open to all primary medical specialties. The second emergency medicine contact was Ben Munger, PhD the founding Executive Director of the American Board of Emergency Medicine, turned consultant. Ben was able to provide advice to AMIA as they negotiated the approval process within the American Board of Medical Specialties. It was at this point that my role at RWJF came into play. RWJF was able to provide the funds to support the development of the core content and the design of fellowship training (Gardner et al., 2009).

In 2013, the first board examination was given with 432 successful candidates becoming the inaugural class of Clinical Informatics diplomates in 2014 (American Medical Informatics Association, 2013). This example demonstrates the pivotal role that philanthropy can play in catalyzing advances in health and health care.

Philanthropy has given me the opportunity to address a broad spectrum of issues with the resources to help make a difference. The plight of those without health insurance had been a long-standing concern of RWJF when I arrived. We sponsored a series of Institute of Medicine studies that clearly demonstrated that people without health insurance lived sicker and died younger than insured counterparts. Cover the Uninsured Week was a central program. The political environment was not conducive for a policy change to provide health insurance for the uninsured so much of our work focused on the enrollment of eligible people in Medicaid and Children's Health Insurance Program (CHIP). My experience at the state level came into good use when recognizing the importance of state-based innovation in the absence of federal engagement. We supported technical assistance to states and encouraged the formation of state-based coalitions of advocates. When the national environment changed and the potential for health reform moved onto the national agenda, Andy Hyman, Director of our Coverage team and I established a strategy to prepare for national policy change. This strategy encompassed a health reform seminar series for Congressional staff and target policy research. Policymakers frequently quoted one study, on the costs of doing nothing, as they deliberated national health reform. After the passage of the Affordable Care Act, the strategy incorporated targeted technical assistance to states to help them implement the complex legislation. Many states remarked that this assistance was instrumental in the development of their health insurance exchanges and implementation of the Medicaid expansion. I believe that our efforts played no small part in the successful enrollment of tens of millions of people into health insurance plans.

In 2014, the Robert Wood Johnson Foundation adopted a new vision, to build a Culture of Health so that everyone in our diverse society can live healthier lives now and into the future (Robert Wood Johnson Foundation, 2018). This new vision gives me an opportunity to fulfill my professional and personal goals of improving the health of this nation in a more comprehensive way. It recognizes that health is more than health and health care but requires engagement of all sectors of society working together with a shared vision of health. While change of this magnitude may take a generation, philanthropy and the Robert Wood Johnson Foundation has the staying power to see it through. As I look forward to continuing to contribute this important movement, I do so reflecting upon the approaches and experiences that have helped me in my career.

My successes in life and my career have been based upon holding fast to personal values and humanistic approaches to management. First, have a moral, ethical and science-based compass. In a political environment it is important to initially identify what the science tells us about the issue. Then find the scientifically supported alternative choices that are morally and ethically appropriate. Finally, use the political process to get as close to the optimal outcome as possible and if you cannot reach an appropriate outcome be ready to move on. Once you start to blur the lines, it becomes hard to tell when you cross them. While I was state health director there were a number of times when I entered meetings with the Governor's office or with legislators knowing where the line was and fully prepared to resign if necessary.

Second, hire good people and then let them do their jobs. While direct engagement in strategic planning and problem solving is critical, the role of senior management is to inspire and lead, not to micro-manage. When I asked Bill Bell, IDPH Deputy Director for Health Care Regulation, why he always brought me such difficult problems, he responded, "the easier ones I handle myself." That is an approach that should be encouraged and nurtured.

Third, the culture of a large organization starts at the top. My highest priority was creating a culture where people felt valued and empowered to innovate and take risks. The most significant personnel problems that I managed involved senior staff who disrespected their employees discouraging reasonable efforts at innovation and risk taking. Senior management must take corrective action and not ignore such practices since the organizational culture would quickly take on the characteristics of the poorly performing manager rather than that one intended.

What counts in life is not the mere fact that we have lived. It is what difference we have made to the lives of others that will determine the significance of the life we lead.

—NELSON MANDELA

References

American Medical informatics Association. (2013). *2013 Clinical Informatics Diplomates*. Retrieved from https://www.amia.org/clinical-informatics-board-review-course/2013-diplomates.

Centers for Disease Control and Prevention. (2017). *Necrotizing Faciitis*. Retrieved from https://www.cdc.gov/features/necrotizingfasciitis/index.html.

Emergency Medicine Residents' Association. (n.d.). *A Brief History of Emergency Medicine Resident Training*. Retrieved from https://www.emra.org/resources/emra-history/a-brief-history-of-emergency-medicine-residency-training/.

Gardner, R. M., Overhage, J. M., Steen, E. B., Munger, B. S., Holmes, J. H., Williamson, J. J., ... AMIA Board of Directors. (2009). Core content for the subspecialty of clinical informatics. *Journal of the American Medical Informatics Association, 16*, 2, 153–157.

Lumpkin, B. (2013). *Joy in the struggle: My life and love*. New York, NY: International Publishing Company.

Lumpkin J. (2001). *Information For Health—A Strategy for Building the National Health Information Infrastructure*. Report of the National Committee on Vital and Health Statistics, Washington, DC. Retrieved from http://www.ncvhs.hhs.gov/nhiilayo.pdf.

Robert Wood Johnson Foundation. (2018). *Culture of Health*. Retrieved from http://www.cultureofhealth.org/.

The History Makers. (2018). *Civic Makers: Frank Lumpkin*. Retrieved from www.thehistorymakers.com/biography/FrankLumpkin.

Wikipedia. (n.d.(a)). *Emmett Till*. Retrieved from www.wikipedia.wiki/Emmett_Till.

Wikipedia. (n.d.(b)). *Fred Hampton*. Retrieved from www.wikipedia.wiki/Fred_Hampton.

Wikipedia. (n.d.(c)). *Harold Washington*. Retrieved from www.wikipedia.wiki/Harold_Washington.

Wikipedia. (n.d.(d)). *Don Detmer*. Retrieved from www.wikipedia.wiki/Don_E_Detmer.

Wikipedia. (n.d.(e)). *Triangle Shirtwaist Factory Fire*. Retrieved from www.wikipedia.wiki/Triangle_Shirtwaist_Factory_fire.

Wikipedia. (n.d.(f)). *Quentin Young*. Retrieved from www.wikipedia.wiki/Quentin_Young.

CHAPTER FIVE

A Darker Shade of Gray

Perpetual Validation of an African American University Administrator

SHERWOOD THOMPSON, EdD

"Leadership has a harder job to do than just choose sides. It must bring sides together."
—JESSE JACKSON

A Little Background

It was a chilly Monday morning on January 7, 1952 in Greenville, South Carolina when I opened my eyes to view a new world, surrounded by my mother and a host of family members. My birth took place at the local hospital, and it was performed by a Black doctor who attended to Black families because the city was segregated. I was told later in life that my father, an enlisted man in the Air Force, held me in his arms and declared that I was going to be an excellent young man when I grew up and I would make something out of my life. That was the last time my mother ever saw him and I never had the opportunity to be held by him again.

My family was delighted to have a new child to raise. It was a practice during those times that the family helped with the upbringing of children. And, for me, it could not have been a better arrangement. I had the best of both worlds, being raised by extended family members. My home life was peaceful, and my childhood was filled with endearing love. I felt secure and that feeling gave birth to a deep stirring inside of me, a longing to accomplish something of importance in life.

I lived in a working low-income family setting. I had no contact with my natural father. Nevertheless, the love and warmth that I received growing up from my family compensated for the lack of a father-son relationship. My uncles and grandfather provided more than the support that I required to be a well-rounded and psychologically healthy boy.

I had the good fortune of living with my grandparents and my aunt, my grandparents' youngest daughter. We all lived, secure, in a small two-bedroom frame house that was filled with love. My grandmother was an enlightened and intelligent hard-working woman who firmly believed in the value of formal education and hard work. She was also an entrepreneur. She had her own domestic business and, despite not having a fancy shop like the Whites had, she faired very well and made an honest living.

Grandmother's educational values influenced my aunt who received her bachelor degree from Morris Brown College in Atlanta and her master's degree from South Carolina State University in Orangeburg, South Carolina. She worked as an elementary school teacher, the music director of her church, and a volunteer who was highly respected in our neighborhood.

Doing well in school was expected and I made it my business to not let my family down even when studying was boring and difficult. I tried to perform to the very best of my ability. Academically I was a "B" student who had a love for books.

Growing up in the Jim Crow South, I was often reminded by family, teachers, neighbors, and churchgoers of the potential horrors of the Jim Crow segregated South. I was acutely aware of the separation between Whites and Blacks. One could not be blind to the segregated culture of the South—the Whites only water fountains, bathrooms and lunch counters were glaring symbols of White supremacy that reminded you, everyday, to stay in your place. Blacks in my hometown were accustomed to sitting at the back of the bus, eating in the back of the lunch counter, and drinking from the Black water fountains. Even the local movie theaters catered to mostly White patrons, with the exception of one or two movies that allowed Black patrons to sit in the balcony.

Seeing the world through young eyes and knowing something was wrong, but not quite knowing what the problem was, made it abundantly clear that society was separate. The reality of what I saw on television did not match the promise that I heard every Sunday morning in church. I often thought about this dilemma and asked my grandparents, "Why would God allow Whites to have authority, influence and power over Blacks? Why was there such a significant economic disparity of wealth between Blacks and Whites? Why has civilization left Black people out?" They never answered these questions.

Living in a loving family was the saving grace that supported and nurtured my belief in the unlimited possibility that someday I would going to escape from that misery. I wanted a better life for my family and for me. I wanted to pursue my passion and find something distinctive and profoundly useful in life to mask the reality that I found myself experiencing.

At a young age, I was taught by my family that the only alternative to living in a society filled with hate, dire neglect, and the daily, dreadful consequences of being Black in the White man's world which meant experiencing legal limitations imposed on you was to seek a path that would lead to acquiring educational skills and competencies. I heard it over and over from my family and friends, "once you get some education, they could never take it away from you." I was told that a college degree would not end racial hatred, but it would give me more professional options. It was thought to be the ticket out of hell. Armed with this information and encouragement, I set out at an early age on my personal quest to become an educated person.

As a student attending an all-Black elementary, junior high, and high school, what mattered to me was getting the training that would free me from the chains of oppression. In an all-Black educational setting, I was immersed in daily motivational lessons about life from Black teachers who felt it was their appointed duty to teach the curriculum and, of course, to teach lessons on how to survive life in the racially divided South.

As history would have it, I lived in the same neighborhood and attended the same high school as Rev. Jesse L. Jackson, founder of the Rainbow/PUSH Coalition. The neighborhood in which he lived was Haynie Street and I lived on Dixon Avenue not too far from his house, a section of the Black community near the downtown business district in Greenville, South Carolina. Rev. Jackson, as a teen, was a favorite athlete of mine. He was ten years older than me and a celebrity homeboy so we never encountered each other. Nevertheless, we had many of the same teachers in high school and they made it their business to admonish younger Black boys to be like Jesse. That encouragement seemed to be a theme at Sterling High School.

Before transferring to the White high school attended Sterling High School until the fall of 1968. At that time, I transferred to the all-White Greenville Senior High School under the Freedom of Choice School Desegregation Plan. The local National Association for the Advancement of Colored People (NAACP) and Black churches were encouraging families to take advantage of the plan because it provided the integration of schools in states that had a segregated educational system by letting Black and White students integrate by their own choice. Only the poorer White families allowed their children to attend all-Black schools while very few Blacks, except a merger number of Black middle-class families, elected to send their children to all-White schools under the plan.

My family urged me to attend Greenville Senior High School, the all-White school just blocks from my home. Attending this school changed my life forever. Almost immediately upon enrolling in this previously all-White High School, I observed that White students were not as smart as I had been led to believe they were. I also noted that the White teachers were not as knowledgeable as those dedicated Black teachers that I had at Sterling High School. There was always an occasion to talk about what it was like to be a Black person attending a White high school. Black individuals and Whites alike gave me their undivided attention whenever I was asked to compare my Black school experience with that of my White school experience.

Attending the White high school focused unwanted attention on me; people were curious about my experiences. One such experience occurred one evening when I was walking home from band practice. A car load of White teens kept driving by and shouting insults at me. I walked on, planning certain routes that I would take if they stopped to confront me. They never stopped, and instead drove by, threw beer bottles at me, and sped off.

I became very popular at the White high school among Black and White students. With the exception of a few Black and White students who refused to get along, I thought the relationship between the races was civil. I did my school work and did the best I could. I was a member of the high school marching band, I was a drummer, and I also drove two school bus routes.

Congress passed the 1968 Civil Rights Act when I was a junior in high school. This landmark legislation tackled discrimination in housing and made it a federal crime to, "by force or by threat of force, injure, intimidate, or interfere with anyone … because of their race, color, religion, or national origin" (1968). The local NAACP became very active in promoting equal opportunities in housing and employment cases. I got caught up in the crossfire between living a carefree life as a teenager and being empathic to the Civil Rights Movement. It became apparent to me that I had to set my sights on helping "my people" and advocate for their human rights.

I attended community meetings, mostly in Black churches, that discussed civil rights issues. I became friends with Black and White adults who were staging civil rights challenges to local Jim Crow laws. In the Deep South, it took fourteen years after the famous Brown v. Board of Education Supreme Court decision before southern states introduced the Freedom of Choice School Desegregation Plan. Local attention to human rights started me thinking about developing a new game plan in life.

I became a favorite among individuals attending civil right meetings and gatherings. My passion for helping Black people was obvious, and many professional adults were very comfortable discussing organizational strategies with me and asking me for my opinion. I felt important. No matter how dangerous it was to meet and plan civil disobedience events, I made a conscious decision to make a profound commitment to participate in the civil right movement.

I did not know that there would be a hefty price to pay for my involvement. I first became aware that the movement would exact a price on my life when the local owner of a business that I worked for fired me and restricted me from ever returning to the property. I was surprised and I asked the owner, with whom I had developed an excellent working relationship over the three years that I worked there, why he decided to fire me. He only said, "It's a shame that you got involved with the civil rights mess."

Upon being elected President of the Youth NAACP organization in 1969, a news story with my picture appeared in the local morning newspaper. At the time, I had a morning bus route in a working class White neighborhood, driving White elementary school children to school. I was naïve to the fact parents of the children were going to react negatively to my new role as President of the Youth NAACP. I found out about their disgust with me one morning when I was making my rounds through their neighborhood. Not one child, out of about 45 children who regularly rode my bus, boarded the bus that day. They did not return for over a week. There were calls from the parents to school officials to fire me and replace me with a White driver. However, the school officers did not fire me, they supported me. My supervisor told me to continue driving my bus route each morning and eventually the White parents would allow their children back on the bus.

Sure enough, on the last day of the first week, I picked up one little elementary school girl standing in front of her house with her mother. Her mother apologized for the behavior of her neighbors and told me that she was not afraid to allow her daughter to ride with me because she trusted me and believed that no harm would come to her daughter. I thought to myself: "Harm, me harm your daughter, that thought never crossed my mind." But most of the White parents felt that having a Black bus driver, who was connect with the NAACP would be a danger to their children. Imagine, they thought that I was going to convert to a violent monster, like the Black face actor who chased a White woman in the 1915 movie, *The Birth of a Nation*. That next Monday, all 45 children were back on the bus, and their confusion about why they were not allowed to ride my bus was just as perplexing as my naïveté had been.

Sit-ins, marches, outdoors protest rallies, speaking engagements, and debate on the virtues of equal rights were my new responsibilities. This leadership experience culminated with an invitation to testify with other young Black students before the Senate Select Committee on Equal Educational Opportunity of the

United States Senate, Ninety-First Congress, Second Session on Equal Educational Opportunity in 1970. Senator Edward Brooke of Massachusetts, the only Black Senator in Congress at the time, was a member of the Senate Select Committee. After the hearings, he dispatched a member of his staff to interview me and to encourage me to consider attending the University of Massachusetts in Amherst. In the words of the Senate aide, "The Senator wants you to help desegregate the University of Massachusetts." I was shocked. I replied, "Isn't Massachusetts the cradle of liberty? desegregation is not needed in Massachusetts." He laughed and said, "You just don't know."

I attended the University of Massachusetts at Amherst (UMASS) and worked with many state leaders, faculty and students from all cultural backgrounds to bring about full integration at the flagship institution. Later, after graduation, I returned to UMass to assume the position of diversity officer, where I was able to focus on the leadership experiences I had gained in the South during the civil rights movement. I was pleased to know my leadership skills afforded me great success in accomplishing the requirements of the job.

Let me turn my attention to some real cases I experienced as a professional leader working in post-secondary settings. I will share some valuable takeaways I learned during my professional leadership roles on university campuses. These lessons have been useful guiding principles that have helped me to navigate my career in a favorable direction.

I mentioned previously that I was taught early in life to value education. During my professional experiences working in leadership roles on campuses of some of this country's top universities, I was able to acquire excellent education experiences and to learn how to work with diverse populations from around the world.

Introduction

My career started in higher education administration the same year that Microsoft Word was introduced to the world. Unemployment was at an all-time high of over 12 million people. Ethiopia experienced the worst drought in history with over 4 million deaths. I traveled to Addis Ababa, the capital of Ethiopia, to witness first-hand the human suffering of the drought. The world population in 1983 hit an all-time high of 4.7 billion people, and Cabbage Patch Kids were the major gift item on most family's Christmas list (The People History, 2015).

My first position was Director of the Office of Third World Affairs (OTWA) at a major New England public land grant university with a student population of over 18,000. This office was similar to today's institutional diversity operations on university and college campuses. I headed a small staff centrally located in the Student Union building on campus. Prior to accepting the appointment as director of OTWA, I had a successful career managing restaurants in the Deep South.

My memory of that experience is quite vivid. I remember working with colleagues from across the campus who were independent—they worked alone. There was very little collaboration during the first years of my tenure as a diversity officer. Over time, I was successful in developing relationships with key administrators that lead to co-sponsorship of educational awareness programs and diversity training activities. It did not dawn on me until later in my career that the community in which I lived, was made up of individuals from the Northeast who were mostly White and Protestant. These very rigid individuals were figuring out, in their own way, how they were going to work with me. I brought to the position a well-established leadership style that I acquired during my experience volunteering in the post-civil rights era of the 60s. I defined would define that leadership style as servant leadership, and I had a tremendous background working with diverse populations. My relationship with students of color and members of the international community was outstanding.

My first years working in a campus-wide leadership position enlightened me to the culture of a major New England public land grant university. I quickly learned that, in addition to the many variations of bias and discrimination, there existed a very subtle form of discrimination that interrupted the building of potential good relationships. I discovered that there was a deliberate culture among some of my White counterparts, in which they would exhibit an intellectual superiority; some of my White counterparts displayed a harsh intellectual superiority complex.

I experienced this early on in my career while participating in staff meetings or when I attended workshops or professional development training programs. I would express my views, and before I could complete my sentence, my White counterparts would speak up and add to or challenge my statements. I experienced this treatment for quite some time. As with environmental irritants, I learn to adjust to those individuals who often tried to demonstrate that they had more knowledge than I had by letting them talk until they were exhausted from hearing themselves. My approach was a practical one: I asked, from what source did you derive your information and where's the evidence? Often a hush would cover the room, and the meeting was then able to proceed. Very seldom was my question answered.

In spite of the challenges from my White counterparts, I survived and thrived quite successfully. Over time, with some intrusive tactics, I was able to establish great relationships with my White counterparts.

One takeaway from this experience is simply this: Do not get into a shouting match with your colleagues over who knows the most. Say less and let others decide, based on the merit of your performance, what you do or do not know. The evidence of who is the expert will surface in the results of the work that has to be conducted. Say little and do a lot. This tactic gives you an aura of excellence because you are not reacting to someone else's combative personality.

Leadership in Program Development

As director of the Office of Third World Affairs (OTWA), I had the responsibility of establishing educational programs for campus-wide audiences. This responsibility was critical to educating the campus about the issues of multiculturalism and internationalization. Many of the programs that were planned and sponsored were programs with topics ranging from bringing awareness to the campus about the Grape Boycott headed by Cesar Chaves to supporting the free Nelson Mandela movement. The staff of the OTWA decided to plan and execute a long-range "Red Ribbon Campaign in support of the international movement to release Mr. Mandela from prison."

The Red Ribbon Campaign was successful. Tens of thousands of red silk ribbon with copper color safety pins were distributed across New England and on select campuses across the United States. Instructions were sent to campus student organizations as well as community civil and grassroots organizations outlining how to launch a Red Ribbon Campaign. It was our hope that each independent organization would extend that distribution of the ribbons, thus, increasing the widespread awareness of the free Nelson Mandela campaign.

In addition to encouraging individuals to wear the red ribbon, the OTWA, in conjunction with other campus organizations, sponsored educational programs with national and international speakers. The OTWA student group sponsored a film festival to advance the message of the free Nelson Mandela movement. Press releases were sent to local and national media outlets informing them of the meaning and urgency of the Red Ribbon Campaign.

This effort was a call to action to support an international political prisoner. It was the efforts of many campuses and community organizations to bring awareness to an injustice. This global citizenship activity was a collaborative effect to bring national and international stakeholders together for a common cause. This activity encouraged international students living in the United States and the United States native-born citizens to join to bring attention to an unjust practice by a lawless intrusive White government in South Africa. The collaboration resulted in improving international relationships, increasing international travel from the United States to other developing countries, and invigorating international faculty and student exchange programs. This one effort broaden international relations and cooperation among college students and faculty. In effect, this project encouraged several individuals to think about the moral nature of political and social conditions around the globe. International action at home is a global citizenship exercise and while its focus was on the injustices occurring in South Africa, it had a secondary intent, promoting awareness and education emphasis on domestic injustices as well.

A lesson to be learned from this one program was that it is useful and important to engage in issues that are beyond your borders. The outcome of such activities is always far more impactful than one might realize at first. The snowball effect of advocating for a cause larger than oneself can resonate into a major common good. The benefits are tremendous and far-reaching in many ways. In the beginning, it was the hope of the OTWA staff just to impact the campus; however, it did not take long for the campus impact to spill over into the state and beyond.

Working on a project that is larger than life provides stretch opportunities that develop practical connections and positive relationship building. The learned benefit from this project was profoundly discovered after the completion of the campaign. The value of the effort the expense and the hours of work yielded goodwill and positive civic relations with the campus and key stakeholders from around the world. This small effort, with its key issue to bring awareness to the campus about a social and political injustice, eventually proved to have a major impact that crossed cities, states, regions, and nations.

Leadership in Building Community Relations

While working as the director of the institutional diversity office at a large Midwestern university, I learned that one of my responsibilities was to so-sponsor and plan the annual Martin Luther King, Jr. Banquet. This event had a rich history and was a major community and annual campus event.

I was fortunate that my office had one staff member who was familiar with this annual event. Hearing from the staff member about the event was a tremendous help to me, and it gave me ideas as to how the event could be improved.

My office invited campus and community members to form a M. L. K. Banquet Planning Committee. The committee held regular bi-weekly meetings. This aspect of the planning process went well. However, another aspect of the process, one that I will call the invisible planning committee ran interference with the designated community and campus planning committee. This invisible committee was a collection of central university administrators who felt it was their responsibility to advise me on how the event should unfold. They suggested to me that I should make sure that certain conservative speakers were considered instead of the more popular liberal speakers that the planning committee had recommended. This invisible committee also strongly hinted that a certain type of food should be served at the banquet instead of the popular "soul food" menu that the community became accustom to. And, to top it off, these self-appointed invisible planning committee members recommended that I convince the regular planning committee members of the value of these changes to the program. This was the most difficult task that I was expected to perform. As it came from the higher ups in the administration, those who, as you can imagine, would be either a supporter of my career on campus or would be a forceful detractor. This was a dilemma.

The Martin Luther King, Jr. Banquet Planning Committee members were very diverse. They were members of the local government, clergy, school district, business community, and retired educators from the University. Without explaining to them the challenges that the senior university administrators place on me, they openly in one of the meeting cautioned me that I most likely would be approached by the central university administration to make modifications to the banquet program. Announcing this possibility was a relief to me, or perhaps it was reassuring to know that the committee had seemingly experienced this type of manipulation before.

As head of the planning committee and the director of the institutional diversity program on campus, this situation put me in a leadership position which required a delicate balancing act between the community and the campus. On the one hand, I wanted to make sure that the community had the quality banquet that they expected without major modifications from the central administration. On the other hand, I wanted to make sure that I would not bargain away my influence with the central administration on campus where I had my academic and administrative home. I discovered that working with the central administration is akin to playing poker. In the game of poker you have a set number of chips. The player are dealt cards and then during the betting round, the player bet a certain number of chips by placing them in the pot. Now, the way this game is played, if you win, the chips in the pot are yours. However, if you lose, you do not get your chips back.

Working as an administrator on a university or college campus is like playing poker. As the person in charge of the banquet planning, I was acutely aware that the chips I put in the pot, or the decisions that I make, would come back to me in winning fashion if my decisions were accepted by all parties involved, or I would lose my chips and my influence and power would be diminished if my decisions were met with opposition.

Luckily, in my situation, the history of the program carried with it certain practices. Among those practices were meetings that the community leaders held with the central university administrators, promotion of the event by campus and community co-sponsors, and the general excitement of both the community and the campus about the upcoming event and its relevance to the overall community. In many ways, even though there was pressure coming from the community planning committee and the central administrators, there was also a history of cooperation and solidarity that in the end, the two parties reconciled their differences and the planned event successfully proceeded without controversy.

I learned that this battle of the wits occurred every year and it played out as an exercise of power by both community leaders and campus leaders. The unsuspecting director of the institutional diversity office was the individual that carried the burden during this contest. I also learned that depending on the side that the director took would inevitably determine how effective that person would be as a power broker.

What Are Some Lessons Learned?

When you are involved in coordinating activities that involve internal and external stakeholders, make sure you are not persuaded to take sides or assume a particular point of view. Remember that there will be second-guessers. These second-guessers will try to make decisions for you. And if you let them intervene, they just might create consequences that will make your job difficult and very challenging. The same is true of complainers, persons who, seemingly, you just can't please. Let them have their say, but do not let their criticism influence your well informed decisions.

Be professional, stay out of the gaming environment, let all parties know that you only role is to ensure the highest possible quality and relevant outcome of the event. Furthermore, let all parties know that you are interested in what is best for both the community and the campus and that you believe that the decision that you make are well informed and will satisfy the expectations of both parties. Quite frankly, the hardest thing an administrator will encounter is trying to satisfy all people—it can't be done. Nevertheless, with well-developed goals and reasonable expectations, you will have excellent justification for the actions you take and the decisions you make.

Working with Members of Your Own Cultural Group

I was very excited about moving to a southern college town to work for a major National Collegiate Athletic Association (NCAA) division one research university. Knowing the South has a large number of people of color, was a positive lure for me and I was quite giddy about make the transition from the Midwest to the South.

My reception upon arriving at the campus was very encouraging. Members of the local community invited me to community events; they introduced me to key leaders, and we communicated and developed excellent relations. The same was true for the campus community. Students, faculty and the administration welcome me with open arms. I was quite pleased with all the attention.

Immediately, with the help and partnership of community leaders, my office organized educational programs that addressed the needs of the campus and the community. The staff of the institutional diversity office conducted a series of research activities to determine what the needs and aspirations of our client groups were. We gained valuable information by conducting focus groups. We captured insightful information from surveys we sent out to the campus community and daily formal and informal conversations with campus and community individuals were also extremely useful.

All of the activities and programs that were sponsored by the institutional diversity office were research based and in most cases, they were piloted before we publicly launched them. We were riding high with success and notoriety.

Then changes took place on campus about diversity programs. The university legal office informed me that certain long-standing diversity programs would be cut, and some would be suspended. The reason for this action was to make sure the university did not appear as if it was providing minority set-asides to faculty and students.

The successful faculty recruitment and retention grant was cut, minority scholarships were suspended, and resources provided to the institutional diversity office were monitored. The thinking by the legal office was that only programs that had a broad base purpose could be implemented. The tension was high and of course, there was great confusion about what we could and could not do. There was even talk about eliminating the university institutional diversity office altogether.

The university legal office was making decisions for the university based on a very cautious and narrow premise that all activities and programs that provided resources to persons of color were in violation of court rulings on race and college admission. In reality, what the legal office's motive was, and they admitted as such, was to satisfy conservatives who oppose racial preferences.

The civil rights community, churches, social justice organizations, and leadership of the university stood up for equal rights for faculty and students of color. It was decided that the legal office, in all good faith, may have been too narrow in their interpretation of the law. The decision was made by the central administration to continue to provide limited resources to expand opportunities to persons of color working at and attending the University.

This decision was the tipping point for the institutional diversity office and it influenced the type of programs we sponsored and the type of activities we engaged in. One such activity was a simple research project that showed, each semester, the academic and racial profile of students admitted to the university. We would conduct a comparison of the College Board scores that undergraduate students were entering the university with—class rank, GPA, SAT scores, etc. The College Board works to "promote excellence and equity in education." To our amazement, we discovered that over fifty percent of White students were being admitted as transfer students. Black student were entering the university with impressive College Board ranking but it appeared as if the White students who transferred to the university did not have to possess the same academic standards that the vast majority of Black students possessed.

The institutional diversity office held a press conference and shared our findings with the general community. The findings were very sobering, indeed, and many individuals' especially White faculty members found it hard to believe that the vast majority of the Black undergraduate students' academic backgrounds were superior to those of their White transfer student counterparts. The alarm went off and these findings were the talk of the campus and community.

The University has a well-established African American Studies Department with celebrated faculty. One afternoon, several paid an unannounced visit to my office to talk with me. Knowing most of the faculty that were in the group, I was delighted to host their visit. The lead faculty, I believe he was the chair of the department, quipped that I was stirring up a mess on campus. A second, younger male faculty member interrupted the senior faculty member and said outright, with a nervous voice, that I was making things bad for Black people on campus by exposing the data that my office had discovered. After his comments, there was a roar of voices agreeing and disagreeing with his verbiage. I quieted the group down and tried to reason with them and come to some mutual ground. However, the majority of them were bent on believing that the "White folks" were going to penalize Black people on campus for exposing the disparities between Black and White students' enrollment profiles.

I thought this was a very uncommon display of antebellum reaction by Black academicians. The thought that somehow, they and other Black staff and faculty on campus would experience backlash because one office revealed public information was mind-blowing. Undoubtedly, they believed that the post-civil rights era concretely had not changed White attitudes towards Blacks. It's a preposterous though that intellectuals would express irrational fears about conservative reaction to the truth about enrollment data pointing to Black students academic achievement. These pseudo-Black militants were in fact patronizing their White counterparts. They bowed to the power structure and seemingly forgot about the power of alliance and togetherness among individuals from the same cultural group.

When the delegation of Black faculty left my office, I thought of the work of Dr. Harold Cruse the author of the book, *Plural but Equal*, when he mentioned that Blacks were expanding the class stratification and that "professional advancement by upwardly mobile Blacks in both private and public sectors only demonstrated, it was implied, that racism a was becoming less and less a real barrier against Blacks ..." (p. 286). I assume that the Black faculty admonishment to me was a kind of warning that I was somehow missing up the notion that all persons are created equal.

The lessons learned from this situation were painful, yet very instructive. On a predominately White university campus, one would hope that there would be a support groups of members from your cultural group willing to lend their backing and empathy. However, in that case, it appeared that they were intent on eclipsing and circumventing the work that shone a spotlight on Black student academic achievement. There is no telling how many of their White counterparts they tried to convince that the research on Black student academic achievement was not relevant to the discussion of equal opportunity on campus.

The ramification that members of your same cultural group would expect that you will not essentially tell the truth about and reflect on the facts about the student of color achievements means only one thing; that reluctantly, there comes a time when the ethics of truth must prevail over the consensus of individuals who have their selfish agenda. You must be comfortable with credibility and leaders must be comfortable with themselves. Leaders will often face criticism from members of their cultural group. Some of the criticism might be negative, and some might be the selfish agenda of someone who simply want be have solo status on campus.

Never allow yourself to be looked on by others as outwitted and petty. Raise above criticism and be undaunted by mean spirited conversation. Be courageous and stand up for your beliefs.

The Balance between Agreeing to Participate and Not Agreeing to Get Involved

As an administrator on a college or university campus your life will be filled with lots of meetings, events, and crises. Often, as an administrator, one wonders if there is enough time in the day to complete assignments, attend to matters related to advancing your career and have a home life. These many agendas can be managed smoothly as long as you put your priorities in order.

On a regional campus in the central part of the country there were very few academic leaders of color on campus and even fewer professionals of color living in the surrounding community. The results of this scarcity of persons of color on campus resulted in me being the point person for diversity. I was invited, it seemed on every search committee, every planning committee and every program, event, and activity on campus. I was not too impressed with these invitations. Somehow, I knew that they were framed in a way that screamed that we need you to give color to this group, this program or campus activities. If I accepted all of these invitations, I would not have any time for myself or family. However, if I routinely turned these invitations down, I would get a reputation for being uninterested in helping out the university.

I tried to balance these many invitations and requests. I was very visible on campus and made a significant contribution to campus life. Nevertheless, the more I contributed to activities and committees as well as other campus service opportunities, the greater the number of invitations I would receive to participate. There were times that I would work through lunch and carry tons of work home just to keep up. One thing for sure, when you agree to help others, very few people will be in your corner to help you. And in most cases, when you are the expert in your field, it's hard to locate the appropriate person to assist you with your work.

I had to wrestle with the question of how I would contribute to the campus as a member of committees and other activities and make sure that I would be successful in completing my assignments. One such case involved a vice president who encouraged faculty and professional staff to attend sports events to assist the campus police with monitoring for alcohol consumption. The university policy prohibited open containers at sports events. So, students would smuggle their favorite drink into the games.

The vice president would send an email asking individual staff to volunteer at sports events. I made the decision that since I was overcommitted during the day assisting in a broad array of campus activities and events, then, maybe, opting out of playing police at the sports games would be understandable. I spoke with the vice president and shared my professional decision and felt that he fully understood my position. Oh, was I wrong.

Over the course of the semester, as I would come in contact with this vice president, I begin to sense a feeling of distance from him. I noticed that he was not the same smiley, friendly person he once was. Sensing the difference in his behavior, I realized that since I did not respond to his request in the way that he wanted me to respond, I was beginning to experience his disapproval. This attitude carried on throughout the semester and spilled over into the summer months as well. At one time I thought I would confront this person. However, I decided not to make an issue out of something he had already developed. I took the typical route and said nothing to him about my observations.

This vice president was not done with his attitude toward me. He actually would mention me in conversations with his staff and colleagues, many of whom were my professional friends also, and tell them how I refused to help the university. The reports came back to me from my professional friends and of course, I knew that I was being ostracized. Now one thing I learned early in my career is that senior academic leaders can make your life easy or can make your life hell on a campus. What they say has great weight, and whether it is true or false, their word will have greater credibility than your word.

While faculty, professional staff and students knew that I was intensely involved in all kinds of campus activities and committee work, there were some who felt that somehow I betrayed the university by not participating in volunteering to work sports events.

I worked hard to establish a successful relationships with my colleagues and even with the vice presidents. Thus, to suggest that things improved with the vice president would be to fabricate the truth. Every strategy I employed to patch up the situation failed.

Lessons learned from this situation were invaluable. I learned that it would have been better for me to negotiate with the vice president, agreeing to attend some sports games in place of serving on committees and working at student events. There's no hard and fast rule as to the number of committees, events, and activities you serve on, no policy that outlines what one should do if you refuse to serve on one committee at the neglect of another committee or service activity. There is no substitute for negotiation. By establishing some mutual expectations, I believe I could have defused some of the misunderstandings that erupted from not accepting one assignment, even though I was inundated with serving on others.

The other lesson learned from this experience is always to communicate clearly. Do not let you failure to speak up in an appropriate manner hinder your relationships with your colleagues. Discuss how you would approach a situation and give suggestions on how situations can be handled by using other options. Communicate your situation and the gravity of your responsibilities in a clear and persuasive manner. Seek understanding from your audience and request an agreement that your recommendations will be honored without retribution. Accomplishing clear communications can prevent misunderstandings, and it can help you prevent future problems with colleagues, especially those with higher level positions.

Conclusion

One of the main lessons that I have learned during my tenure in academic administrations is the lesson that teaches individuals not to insult other people. This lesson has its roots deep within the truism of the "Golden Rule." This lesson is a witness to the need for stronger ethics and respect for educational leaders and educators. Society and even college and university campuses are forgetting this truism.

This discussion deliberated my professional experiences working in a select numbers of educational environments that provided me with profound learning experiences. I call these experiences lessons learned. Throughout my professional career I have amassed progressive experience serving as the Institutional Diversity Officer for three Carnegie Foundation Division-I Public Research Universities, one Polytechnic University, and one regional campus at which I have gained tremendous insight and knowledge into the culture and nature of a university setting. I have a successful record of scholarship, teaching, and service/community engagement. I have been recognized for my work with international schools and colleges in China, India, and East Africa. I have distinguished myself through successfully working with regional and national educational associations, as well as federal, state, and local governmental agencies. Currently, I am the President of a national educational research association, and serve on national boards, committees and review panels. At this writing, I am the interim chief diversity officer for a medium sized regional comprehensive university. In every case, depending upon the nature of the service that I am involved in, I take the aforementioned lessons learned with me to help navigate my professional involvement within educational organizations.

The one major thing that I have learned from my progressive experiences, is that it is better to do more listening than to do more talking. I am a listener. My professional experiences taught me to develop relationships with a vast constituency. I have benefited greatly from my professional network of colleagues and friends.

I have had extensive experience working with and promoting diversity within university communities. The hallmarks of my contributions in promoting diversity have been creating innovative recruitment strategies for persons of color, comprehensive institutional diversity plans, best practices in early intervention programming, university ombudsman on issues of institutional diversity and inclusion, and the development of programs for creating and implementing civility and a wholesome campus climate that honors, respects, and encourages institutional diversity. This work on college and university campuses is paramount to creating a healthy and intellectually stimulating campus environment.

I transitioned after two decades working in the diversity arena as a full-time professional administrative to the faculty and have assumed academic responsibilities. I hold the faculty rank of tenured full professor, my academic home is in the College of Education, and I am active in research and scholarly endeavors. In the academic arena, I have served as Assistant Dean of a College of Education, Director of a Teacher Education Services Office, Executive Director of a K-12 Laboratory School, and Chief Diversity Officer. The lessons as mentioned earlier were lessons learned and served as the guiding light for my success in these positions.

Just as no two human fingerprints are alike, there are no two higher education institutions alike. Recognizing this uniqueness, I have worked to enhance the human capital of educational enterprises. The stories that I shared all factor into the exclusive need for human dignity and ethics in higher education programs. The campus environment is the breeding ground for young intellectuals and they require a careful recognition of the importance of human interactions. I maintain that individual leaders on college and university campuses can model these aforementioned guiding principles and learned lessons that position them to be effective and successful educators. I found out that all it take is a reflective approach to leadership—common perceptions, trust and effective communication that respects individuals and does not berate them.

References

Cruse, H. (1987). *Blacks and Minorities in America's Plural Society: Plural but Equal.* New York, NY: William Morrow.

The People History: Where People Memories and History Join. (2015). The year 1983 from the people history. Retrieved from http://www.thepeoplehistory.com/1983.html.

CHAPTER SIX

Black Male Leadership

Preparing for the Hit in the Gut

KEITH B. WILSON, PhD, MEd

> *"Impossible is just a big word thrown around by small men who find it easier to live in a world they've been given than to explore the power they have to change it. Impossible is not a fact. It's an opinion. Impossible is not a declaration. It's a dare. Impossible is potential. Impossible is temporary. Impossible is nothing."*
>
> —Muhammad Ali

The changing demographics in school systems across the United States is an indication that the diversity in leadership both in higher education and public health is critical. Relative to education, in order to best prepare students who will face increasingly diverse classrooms and clientele, it is important to understand common career paths that many black males have navigated throughout their lifetime. Family, friends, successes, challenges and other variables are all a part of who we are and how we may ultimately deal with systems and the people within these systems. Given this backdrop, this chapter will explore opportunities and successes that have lead me down a career path that I consider exciting and worthwhile. I will conclude with advice on how to progress despite the many barriers faced in the pursuit of lifelong learning and personal satisfaction in a career in higher education.

Life and Career Influences and Career Path

Introduction

While I will be myopic in focus and primarily address perceptions of my influences including both failures and successes, many of the concepts in this chapter can be generalized to other groups and situations for maximum benefit. Being a Black male can be tough for various reasons that we do not have the time to specially devote in this chapter. More importantly, it is well known that certain groups tend to suffer from mental health concerns more than other groups in the United States. As I am reflecting on my humbled journey, it is important to note that many Black males may have similar barriers and ways of dealing with those barriers that may prove beneficial for other Black males coming behind us in the academy. Thus, I am hoping that this chapter can be instructive and provide a glimpse in both the commonalties and contrasts in experiences that many Black males face growing up in a system that might not value what we can contribute to the academy and the larger society.

Given the current and changing demographics in the United States, it is important to continue seeking diversity (i.e., people & thinking) in many professions. For example, in education and health, women generally make up the majority of employees. At the moment, women comprise a significant amount of the educational services population (e.g., elementary & secondary schools, trade school training) in the United States. In the area of social services and health care, there is even a higher proportion of women and people who are part of underrepresented groups employed (Bureau of Labor Statistics, 2010). Thus, it not surprising that many of my influences early in life came from two people in my household that represented both education and human services. Indeed, "The changing demographics present human service providers with the added challenge and opportunities of modifying ways to assist a more diverse citizenry" (Wilson, Gines, Gary, & Brown, 2015, p. 252). Yes, the substantial influences of my Mom and Dad.

I was born the oldest out of five children (four boys and one girl) in Spartanburg, SC. In the mid-70s, my family moved to Atlanta, GA when I was twelve years old. Thus, I claim Atlanta as my home when asked, *where are you from?* Being born and raised in the south, the influence of diversity (i.e., race relations) has a lot to do with who I am and the messages I internalized as a kid growing up both in Spartanburg and Atlanta. These environments impacted my parents both in a positive and constructed way. Additionally, these influences are so many that I will only have time to briefly highlight in this chapter as a primer to who I am as a person and the issues and people that modeled a young boy to become who I hope is a well-respected man in his profession and community. Yes, influences …

Immediate Family

I have to look no further than my immediate family for many of my profound, yet intense inspirations. As way of background for my parents, my Dad (African American & deceased) was a high school science, math and art teacher and my Mom (African American) was a Social Worker. She retired as a Nutrition Director of Head Start in 2008. My siblings and I had the pleasure of being raised by supportive, firm and intellectually gifted parents. Such as, my Mom was a high school honors student in her hometown of Columbus, GA. My Dad was both very smart and athletic. For example, both the Green Bay Packers and United States Army drafted him around the same. However, my Mom reported that he had to forgo his professional football career and go to the Korean War. As I speculate about the choices my Dad might have had at his disposal during that time in American history, I am not sure if my Dad had a choice in the matter. During a conversation I had with my mom in 2011, I discovered that my Dad was in intelligence when he was in the United States Army. Come to think of it, Dad did not disclose much about his military days or his childhood growing up in Spartanburg, S.C. It was also revealed by my Mom that Dad had an I.Q. around 135. Reflecting on interactions with my Dad during my lifetime, I can honestly say he was the smartest man that I have ever had the pleasure to be around. He could not only help me and the rest of my siblings with our homework, as he and Mom would do, but he could paint, draw and do all sorts of creative things with his hands that others admired. As with many of us, I did not appreciate my Dad's intellectual resources until I was long gone from the home. In summary, my Mom and Dad were great role models for my siblings and me as we were growing up. My parents made sure that we had the mental and emotional means to display our talents in a supportive and loving environment. I consider myself very fortunate in many respects to have had such a supportive parental environment!

Life and Career Influences and Career Path

As is very obvious reading the section about my immediate family, my parents were early contributors to road maps on how to be successful and treat others in a respectful manner. While my parents were early influences in my life and the career path I would follow, others gave me opportunities to expand and test boundaries and or believed in me when I was not as confident in my gifts and talents early in my professional maturation. I truly believe in the adage of hard work and being able to "get people" add to the likelihood of success not only in one's vocational pursuits, but in many components of life. It is indeed an honor to get mentored by those who continue to provide guidance and encouragement and expect nothing but the same from the mentee. No other remuneration was either implicitly or explicitly stated. In summary, the residuals of paying the perils of knowledge, wisdom, support and validation forward has enhanced my life and the life my family for well over three decades.

The first major influencer in my life outside of my immediate family was Mrs. Ruth Beal (deceased). It all started back when I enrolled at Wilberforce University (WU), the first private Historically Black Colleges and Universities (HBCUs) in the United States, to pursue my Bachelor's degree in Rehabilitation Services. Early spring of my senior year, I was asked by the senior professor and coordinator of the Rehabilitation Services Program whether I had thought about pursuing graduate studies. The person who posed this question was no other than Mrs. Ruth Beal. While I pondered the question asked by Mrs. Beal for several seconds which seemed like a lifetime, I must have projected a lack of confidence to the question she asked me. Well, she was right. At that time, I had never considered graduate school once my matriculation at WU had concluded. In retrospect, the expression that Mrs. Beal observed was the look of someone considering the many horror stories about graduate school I had heard from countless upper classmen at WU. Secondly, while I met with a lot of academic success at WU, I still wondered if I had the intellectual ability to complete the academic rigors required to earn a graduate degree. After my long and uncomfortable pause, Mrs. Beal looked at me and immediately said the following. "Keith, you did really well in all of my classes and you have the smarts to make it in graduate school." Yes, I still remember her direct words to me thirty-two years later. However, I did not know at the time, what happened next would change my life forever. After a polite acknowledgement of Mrs. Beal referencing my demonstrated intellectual talents, she continued by saying she was going to make a call to Kent State University (KSU) and see if she could get me an interview in their Rehabilitation Counseling graduate program. At the time, the KSU had one of the highly ranked programs in the United States in Rehabilitation Counseling, my chosen field of study. Well, she made the call to the Director of the program (Dr. Martha Walker, retired), I had a successful interview and was accepted into the program at KSU for the following fall semester, three weeks after graduating from WU. I could not have attended KSU without some financial assistance to off-set costs associated with graduate studies.

To my surprise, I was also able to compete for and receive a financial scholarship during the time I attended graduate school at KSU. While I am not sure where I would have ended up if not for the intervention of a super supporter like Mrs. Beal, having people in your life to see things in you that one might not be able to see in themselves was one of the first pivotal points in my academic career. While my parents and teachers validated and supported me during my early academic experiences, many times this support was not enough to catapult me to the next level. I have much gratitude for all of the Mrs. Beals' in the world who mentor and instill a willingness to take risks. They build upon an existing foundation and create eagles who soar high above the plains of normal. Indeed, this kind of validation might be viewed as a special calling that will touch many lives though the act of "paying it forward."

Another seminal person in my professional and personal life I would like to highlight is Dr. Roland B. McFadden. Once I completed my studies at KSU in December 1985, I applied for several jobs across the United States. Fortunately, I selected Savannah State College now Savannah State University (SSU) in Savannah, Georgia, which is located in South Georgia and is also an HBCU. The person who hired me was Dr. Ronald B. McFadden, then the Director of the Developmental Studies Department at SSU. He is presently the Director of the Ronald McNair Program at the University of Tennessee-Knoxville, where he has been employed for close to twenty-five years. At the time, I remember appreciating his willingness to hire and give me an opportunity to grow at SSU. While Dr. McFadden departed SSU for the University of Tennessee Knoxville after my second year, we eventually became close friends and I consider him a close friend and confidant to this day. I learned many things from Dr. McFadden. For instance, Dr. McFadden related to people in every walk of life with the constancy of disposition that ensured respect and appreciation from many he has helped over the years. I also learned the application of student-centered mentoring for all students, in particular for those who may be part of underrepresented groups. Thus, my relationship with the Ronald McNair and Upward Bound Programs, for example, continue to this day with my participation as a research, social and workshop presenter almost thirty years later. I indeed owe a lot to this particular person for giving me an opportunity to grow and expand during my most formative years as a young professional. Additionally, he was and continues to be one of the smartest men I have had the pleasure to meet. He is an exemplar of what intelligence and empathy projects. While I do not know how many he has mentored, his dedication to life and meeting challenges head on will continue to be his calling card long after he has vacated the walls of the academy. Without hesitation, the social, academic and progressive fruit he produced are many and will continue to yield sweet nectar!

Career Path

As mentioned before, my Dad was a high school science, math and art teacher for many years. Undeniably, teaching has been in my bloodline for a long time. Fortunately for me, I just happened to stumble on what I have spent the majority of my career doing, teaching, research and service. While my interests in psychology and sociology in the earlier stages of my vocational and academic career influenced my career, my dad influenced my teaching almost serendipitously. There are times I can remember going to schools my dad taught at and interacting with his students and colleagues. Dad taught at the high school and he was stationed at the front gate taking tickets to get into the football games on Friday nights. I digress. Accordingly, when I found myself teaching a class at the collegiate level when I was 23 years old as part of the job of Counseling Coordinator/Psychometrist in the Developmental Studies Department, I could not deny my pedigree and creative pedagogy in the educational environment. I found myself wanting to pursue higher education and teaching as I began to get more exposure at SSU. As I recall the many conversations around the dinner table growing up, these were indeed great times for learning not only for myself, but for my brothers and sister as well. While many of my siblings are in different fields from accounting to technology, it is clear that we were all influenced by Dad and Mom in pursuing a particular way of expressing our vocational talents.

Successes

A coined definition of success is an outcome that one might perceive as good or favorable. Using this definition, I have been fortunate to have several categories of career success in my lifetime from degree attainment to administrative opportunities that I was recruited for both within and outside of the university. The most recent career success is being the former Dean of the College of Education and Human Services at Southern Illinois University Carbondale (SIUC). I have earned. B.A., M.Ed., and Ph.D. degrees from Wilberforce University (1984), Kent State University (1985), and The Ohio State University (1997), respectively. I was a center director, a program chair and a full professor at The Pennsylvania State University (PSU) a major research university, The Pennsylvania State University (PSU) all within 15 years of entering the academy as a tenure track faculty member. During my time at Penn State, I created and became owner and Director of Counseling, Consultation and Psychotherapy Services (CCPS) in State College, PA. CCPS was involved in executive coaching, psychotherapy and training and development. I maintained this business for eight years before coming to SIUC as Dean. Additionally, I have been fortunate to win several local, state and national research and service awards in my field. Most recently, I have been honored with two lifetime achievement awards. I have truly been blessed thus far in my career with well over a decade left in my formal academic career before I consider retiring.

Another success that I attribute to both my mom and dad is the unselfish motivation to give back in both financial and non-financial ways to my professional and personal communities. My entire professional academic career has been geared toward paying it forward much as I observed my parents doing as I was growing up. Additionally, the selfless service that I observed by Dr. Ronald B. McFadden, and others, reinforced my commitment to give back in ways viewed as going beyond the call of duty, as noted in one of my formal faculty evaluations. For example, I have been involved in Upward Bound, Summer Opportunity Research Program (SORP), and McNair programs contributing as a workshop presenter, social, and research mentor for the past 29 years. These programs are in place to facilitate college and/or graduate school success for students from underrepresented populations. I view the involvement in many of my professional and social organizations as an extension of my student-centered teaching philosophy. Thus, as I have paid it forward with gratitude for the guidance and example of my past mentors, my mentees owe me nothing but to pay it forward as well.

Interpersonally, I have been fortunate to be able to understand the human condition by way of my professional training as a licensed counselor and the inherent way I view the world and the people and systems connected. As a result, people have commented that they really enjoy working with and for me over the years. When everything is all equal, and I cannot recall when everything is ever all equal, my retention rate of people that I hire tends to be very high. In fact, I can remember when one employee I hired was offered a job that paid more money. That employee shared that they decided to stay because, the work environment that I tended to create offered consistent validation, respect and recognition, which was enough to stay and forego the extra money. Yes, this was surprising for me to hear. Of course, if this employee was offered 50% more money, I am sure the ending might have been different but that's an assumption, I don't know for sure.

Failures

Indeed, I have had several failures. However, I have learned more from my failures than my successes, I think. ... In contrast to success, one definition of failure might be a result that was not satisfactory. Of course, both successes and failures are in the eyes of the beholder as people try to write their own narratives of professional and personal benchmarks. Give what I view as failures, I have several to highlight.

Hiring Personnel (early in career). I was drafted/recruited into administration at an early age by virtue of my job responsibilities at Savannah State University in 1986. However, becoming the person responsible for hiring and firing brought a host of administrative concerns at the young age of 26. Given the opportunity to head/lead a center (Director of Counseling Services, previously known as the Student Support and Retention Services) and hiring the personnel associated with it as its first director was quite interesting and exciting. I committed to not only helping students, but young professionals as well so they could gain a foothold in the door of employment at the college. In the five years as center director, I was able to hire several administrative assistants primarily focusing on the typical match between skill sets and job requirements. Unfortunately for me, I also paid a fair amount of attention to facilitating opportunities for people who had communicated to me that they would be in the position for one year or less if I hired them. In hindsight, it was definitely not a good idea to hire personnel under these circumstances for the following reasons:

1. Training three new administrative assistants in five years was draining on the center and on me. It was not good resource management.
2. The consequences of training new personnel meant, by extension, inefficiency and the loss of rapport with others in the center over time.

Once I departed from the college and was employed in other administrative positions, this hiring practice stopped and I was able to add value once I was on hiring committees for staff, faculty, students and administrators. This was indeed a great learning experience. Again, you can learn a great deal from your perceived failures. Being attentive to resource management is critical in making an informed decision for hiring divisions.

Hiring Personnel (later in career). Another skill acquired is being able to tap into a more qualitative paradigm when making decisions. Some may call this qualitative paradigm your intuition (gut) in order to make informed decisions about personnel. I can recall hiring a person that my gut said not to hire and my head said, why not hire. It turned out that I should have paid more attention to environmental cues that indicated tendencies towards dishonesty and a lack of integrity. However, the person had a very useful skill set I needed on my staff. The follow-through could have been better on my part. It was a great learning experience. I no longer make this same mistake with direct reports.

As life will teach us from time-to-time, being able to pick-up on non-verbal behavior is a key ingredient to success in hiring, promoting and developing a good team of people around you for the ultimate goal of advancing strategic initiatives within and outside of your purview as an administrator, colleague and friend. It is also important to understand your mistakes and be able to recover from them as ways of improving how and what you do in the future. I am not sure where I heard this quote but it goes like this: Life is a great teacher by way of giving you the exam before you have had the opportunity to receive the lecture.

Reflections

As I reflect on my personal and professional life, it is clear that many of my successes were marked by ups and downs that we all can expect to encounter in this roller coaster called life. If I am part of the successful black male linage in the academy. To what do I attribute such success? Well, this is a very easy question to answer for a person who get people and understand systems and history.

Preparing for the Hit in the Gut

Plain and simple, I attribute much of my success in the academy and in life to the perception of "waiting for the other shoe to fall" and/or understanding that, depending on your environment, you will encounter a "tax" that you will have to pay more sooner than later. The "tax" is conceptual and depends on the context in which you might be perceived as being part of an underrepresented group in the workplace, for example. Meaning, in any given fluid situation that involves interactions with people, you can find yourself representing a person who is part of an underrepresented group. Let's say, in the area of education (e.g., elementary, secondary), a female might not be considered underrepresented because of the sheer numbers that females represent in education. On the other hand, being a female in the area of science might be enough justification to include being female as part of an underrepresented group based on the number of females in the science area. The same could be true if we looked at the number of administrators in education at the superintendent and principal levels based on the number of females in administration. Females could be considered part of an underrepresented group in this context as well. In many cases, this "tax" is both perceptual (e.g., antidotal) and factual (e.g., empirical studies indicating discrepancies when other variables are controlled). It is my belief that success is contingent upon several variables, one being understanding people and environments in order to successfully negotiate possible pitfalls and protecting your mental and physical health. In some cases, being part of an underrepresented group might be fluid.

Certainly, the tax I am referring to is the tax that many who are part of underrepresented groups (e.g., gender, sexual orientation, ethnicity, race, disability &

socioeconomic status) are familiar with paying. The first question is how would one know if he or she is paying or will pay a variable of discrimination tax? While there are many ways I could explain the tax concept, I will be ephemeral in my explanation. The first giveaway is when you hear something like the following from one of the aforementioned groups: a. I/We have to work harder to get similar benefits to people who are _____. b. Why do people assume I am not as qualified as _____ just because I am, for example, Female/Gay/Latina. Whether people see the tax as perceptual and/or factual, supported by evidence, it is important to prepare for a higher level of counterproductive attention in order to continue one's productivity and professional ascension to reach a higher career trajectory. This is where the phrase, as in the title of this book chapter, *preparing for the hit in the gut*, comes from.

Preparing for the hit in the gut. Yes, as people who consider themselves as part of underrepresented groups in the United States, it is essential that protecting yourself physically and more importantly in many cases, psychologically. Stay with me. Many of us have gotten hit, accidentally, in the stomach. We remember the hit as painful and many times, may result in a broken rib (s) or just takes our breath away and we might fall on the ground for a few minutes, if we are lucky. If we tense our stomach muscles before the hit, we do not feel as much of the impact. Thus, we do not feel as much pain and may not fall to the ground because of our anticipation of the hit. This is what is meant by the, *preparing for the hit in the gut*, phrase comes from. As Jason E. Gines, a good friend of mine has said several times during conversations, "what we anticipate will not hurt us." Here it is. This is what I attribute to much of my success. Understanding that a punch will be thrown either intentionally or unintentionally, and you must prepare for the punch even when you cannot see the punch coming your way. It is my belief that your knowledge of people, systems and the history of our country and your own personal experiences if we are part of underrepresented groups, will dictate if we do not prepare for the punch that we cannot see, not only will we get hurt, but we will tend to stay down longer and may very well get seriously injured. Because of the training of my parents and a few close mentors in my life, I have been successful in preparing for punches that I cannot see, and when hit, I tend to get up quicker and continue because this too is life in context of who we are and our circumstances in this great county we call America.

I must confess, we all can benefit from preparing for the hit in the gut, regardless of any demographic variable that might yield either positive or negative reactions from the society at large. Speaking directly to the mental health domain, it is also important to teach others how to cope when life may throw us a curve and demand that we make lemonade out of the lemon that was thrown our way. I contend that if we are really good, we can make Kool-Aid out of the lemon thrown our way. I do not think I am there yet!

Conclusion

The changing demographics in America are making it a necessity to include more diversity in higher education leadership, in public health and other venues. Successes in my path in the academy can be traced back to my parents who were my first mentors and influenced my siblings and me beyond words in things we should do in order to be effective in both our personal and professional lives. Additionally, mentors outside of the family are just as influential as we negotiate careers as black males in the academy. We all have a path that we will follow, the question being asked is: When we get to our destination, if we reach the destination, how beat up will we be? Being able to anticipate counterproductive attitudes in the workplace is a way to protect ourselves from potential physical and emotional harm. Creating this kind of cognitive barrier is a good self-defense mechanism for success not only in one's professional career, but personal as well. We do tend to bring work home when we have had a positive or challenging day at the office. Accordingly, how we deal with the stressors of our jobs may dictate the life outside of our chosen vocation as black males.

References

Bureau of Labor Statistics. (2010). *Employed person by detailed industry, sex, race, and Hispanic or Latino ethnicity* (Report No. cpsaat18). Washington, DC: United States Department of Labor. Retrieved from www.bls.gov/cps/cpsaat18.pdf.

Wilson, K. B., Gines, J. G., Gary, K., & Brown, S. (2015). Diversity and multiculturalism among personnel: Hiring, staffing, and supervising an emerging workforce. In: C., Flowers, S. Robertson, & J. Soldner (Eds.), *Counseling supervision and administrative practices in allied health professions* (pp. 247–269). Aspen Professional Services.

CHAPTER SEVEN

How Did I Get Here?

Telling My Story

ADEWALE TROUTMAN, MD, MPH, CPH

"Success is to be measured not so much by the position that one has reached in life as by the obstacles which he has overcome while trying to succeed."
—Booker T. Washington

I've learned over the years that stories have great value. They teach through exposure to the experiences of the storyteller and allow the reader to see possible connections between the teller's presentation and one's own life experiences. In fact it is more enjoyable and potentially more valuable as a teaching tool. Consequently, I'll tell my story and perhaps stimulate someone to see the possibilities in their own lives. It begins with the question "How did I get here?" How did I move from stealing sodas from the corner store to getting one of the strongest anti-smoking ordinances in the country passed and implemented? I know that I have had the privilege of sitting on four national advisory committees for the Secretary of Health and Human Services including Infant Mortality Reduction, Healthy People 2020 and two Institute of Medicine reports. How did I get here?

On March 17, 1946 World War II was over, my father who had been in the Navy came home and I entered the world as the leading edge of the "Baby Boom" generation, that demographic that had been a major force of change in the 60s and the 70s. I was born in the South Bronx and even then it was "the hood". At times, people who meet you or hear about you make certain assumptions about who you are and where you came from. So let me be clear, we were poor. I often say we were *so poor that* we couldn't afford *the or* so we were just *po*. We slept on the roof of our five-story walkup tenement building and lived through the winters, frequently without heat. My brothers and I used to wash and dress standing on chairs over the stove with all burners blasting and the oven pumping.

My neighborhood was all Black and poor. I don't remember ever seeing any white people, or Latinos for that matter, in our hood. My mother had three boys, I was the youngest. My middle brother passed away several years ago. I still at times feel a need to call him on some subject only to recognize that he is no longer alive. My mother always worked and her mother and grandmother helped to keep an eye on us while she supported us. You might ask where was my father during this time. My answer is that I have no memory of his being there including the defining moment in their relationship when he hit my mother. I remember the black eye that contoured her face. And I remember my brothers and I vowing to make him pay for abusing her with a three child army composed of my brothers and me. We were going hit him with heavy wooden stools as soon as he opened the door to come in. We stood behind the door ready to go to war. I eventually got so tired that I went to bed. That was the day that he left. I was 4 and didn't see him again until I was 11.

My oldest brother has told me about instances that involved the heavy use of alcohol and instances of abuse that he witnessed. I know that my father was a cop and I remember hearing a story about his getting involved in a dispute at a local bar that led to his shooting someone. He lost his job because of that, moved to Chicago, and became a long distance truck driver. I often wonder what it would have been like having a father who was involved in my life, offering his wisdom and counsel as I grew, became involved in athletics and with the opposite sex. That was not to be the case.

As I said, I grew up in the hood in a five-story walkup, one of several in our stretch of paradise. I was in the middle of the first grade when my mother moved us to a better neighborhood, still in the South Bronx. This time it was a three-story walkup that almost burned down twice. Well, it was supposed to be a better neighborhood. There was only one white family in our neighborhood and the father was the superintendent, or super as they are usually called. He pulled the garbage and performed other duties. He had a son about my age and we became "friends". Unlike the first hood there were Puerto Ricans in this hood. As a matter of fact, one of them would be my girlfriend in later years. By the way, our "better" hood was known as Fort Apache because it was such a rough neighborhood. There were the Disciples, the Fordham Baldies, the neighbored gangs Teller Ave, the Melrose projects, and Patterson projects and others. We had periodic raids in the hood. The Melrose projects would invade Teller Ave and immediately the Teller guys would beat them up and chase them back to the projects. In retaliation, Teller Ave would raid Melrose. Most people stayed away from Patterson because they had a reputation of being crazy. One night at a party in the projects a serious fight broke out. My friend gave me the nickname, One Punch Troutman.

I was a smart kid who loved to learn but I was painfully shy. I wouldn't speak up in class and didn't interact with the other students. I had been placed in the "smart kids" class throughout my new life in PS35. There was Renssalaer, me and two other black kids. We were in 4-1, 5-1, then 6-1. All the other kids were white. Tracking was and is still real. One good thing about that arrangement was that I got to play the trumpet. I was pretty good at it but remember I was extremely shy. So in Junior High School when it came time to an audition to go into orchestra I was too shy to play and got passed over. In High School that meant you would have to play in the marching band. For football games. I wasn't about to do that when the girls were looking at the football players not the band. Put these facts together with the fact that my mother wouldn't allow me to play football and you got one really disappointed child.

I said I was smart. I had aspirations and dreams back then. I had developed two groups of friends, the white, mostly Jewish, kids from Concourse Ave and further East Bronx my boys from the block. I thought I was something special and had to parcel out my time to make everyone happy. I even played spin the bottle with the white girls with no issues. One day after playing with my Concourse friends someone noticed I was dressed all in Blue. That was cool to me and went I went home I excitedly told my mother that my friend had called me Blue Boy. My mother simply said that she didn't like and that I should be careful. I had no idea what she was talking about and continued to play up there. One Saturday as we often did we were playing ball it Joyce Kilmer Park. I was "in the field "and the other kids were hitting the ball to me. A commotion ensued when one of our friends showed up in the park fresh from his family vacation in Florida. I remember them buzzing around him, anxious to hear about his experiences. I had not started to come in from the field while collecting a ball when I heard in a loud clear voice one of "my friends" said to the traveler, you sure are dark, you're really tan. You look just like a "Nigger". They very quickly said to those gathered around David "Not so loud, he'll hear you." They were talking about me and I still feel the pit in my throat as I write this. That opened my eyes to the ugliness of racism even though I couldn't name it. Needless to say that was the last time I went up there and the idea of having two sets of friends died that day in Joyce Kilmer Park. My mother didn't have to explain her concern over my being called blue boy.

In 1955, when I was nine years old, I had my first taste of terror. We talk a lot about terrorism today referring to masked men with automatic weapons and suicide bombers with names that are not familiar to many of us and who speak in many different tongues. We forget that for African Americans the first "terrorists", the animals that were so abundant, particularly in the south, spoke English, dressed like you and me, practiced Christianity, believed in their superiority were white. They were the Ku Klux Klan (KKK) and their sympathizers' in and out of the southern criminal justice system. In 1955 a teenager from the urban north was sent down south by himself to visit family. This was a tradition that goes way back. It got kids off the street for the summer and gave them a southern and frequently rural experience. So this mother, against her better judgment, sent her son down south to rural Mississippi for the summer. His mother gave him the talk. There is another version of the talk today given to young black males on how to react when stopped by the police to increase their chance of surviving that interaction. The pre going south talk focused on white folk. Don't talk back, even if you are right. Get down on your knees if you have to and beg forgiveness. So, armed with his directions and his teenage judgment coming out of the urban north, Emmet Till was accused of, in some way, disrespecting a white woman. He flirted with, whistled at or did something which a Black male was barred from doing under threat of retaliation. And retaliation and terror was what Emmet got. A gang of whit terrorists went to his relative's house where her was staying and dragged him away from his family and soon after dragged his life from him. Several days later his body was found in the river. He had been severely beaten, one eye poked out and he had been shot. A piece of a cotton gin attached to barbed wire was tied around his neck. Then he was thrown into the river. His mother summed the courage to stand against terror and despite the condition of his body demanded an open coffin so the world could see that savagery of southern racism and to stand up to the terrorist of the southern U.S. On the cover of Jet Magazine was a picture of Emmet in his casket open so that all could see what we were dealing with. I was nine years. I took the copy of Jet Magazine, went down to sit on the stoop, looked at the cover of the magazine and found myself in the coffin with Emmet. I had been south; I was a kid from the urban north who had been terrorized. The message was you don't belong and, as was stated by the Dred Scott decision, Blacks had no rights that a white man had to respect.

Even today I remember heading for the front door of the Howard Johnson's highway restaurant at age 15. I was stopped by the sign the spread across two doors that said "Facilities for whites only". Being a brash 15 year old I said that I was going in anyway. My mother's wisdom held sway that day.

All my assignments in school centered around science. I was in awe of the universe, the planets and the stars. I committed to memory the names of the planets in threes: Mercury, Venus Earth Mars, Jupiter, Saturn, Uranus Neptune, Pluto. What is botany? What are xylem and phloem? What were the names of the dinosaurs? What kind of jet was that that just flew by? My cousins lived near an Air

Force base and they got annoyed at my constantly identifying jets along with a full description of its attributes. I told you I loved science. As a matter of fact I wanted to be an astronomer. Well that dream got no support from JHS 22 Jordan L Mott Junior High School. My other dream was to be a translator at the UN. Now that was really out in Left field. To this day, I have no idea where that came from. There were no role models open to me in either of my dream professions and so that died a slow death. To add insult to injury when it was time to discuss high school with the counselor he told me that I should go to Gompers Vocational School and study to be an auto mechanic. I would have listened to him had I not considered myself to be a superior athlete and Gompers had a terrible basketball team. I told him I was going to DeWitt Clinton High School, one of the basketball powerhouses in New York City and nationally known for the skill of its players. As a matter of fact, the first Division One college team to field an all-Black starting five had two players from DeWitt Clinton High School. That's where I wanted to go. I didn't see that encounter for what it was, namely his committing of a violent act against an aspiring, intelligent Black child that would have had devastating consequences had it been effective. The violence was the destruction of the future of a bright mind and an aspiring psyche that was meant to do great things. How many listened to that direction and never fulfilled his or her potential?

De Will Clinton Was an all-boys high school at that time (1960–63). There were thousands of students from all over New York but mainly from the Bronx and Harlem. Then there were the white kids from other parts of the city. There were often issues between the main groups with name calling and a fight here and there but nothing too serious. Clinton was not a school noted for its academic standing. To me and my friends college was a foreign concept. I don't recall any college prep sessions or visits from colleges to Clinton. It was as if high school was the end of the road. Clinton was known for its athletic teams. The only person that I ever heard of going to college was our top football player on scholarship.

Right next door was Science High School. Do I need to tell you that sports was not a Science High School thing? It made them obvious targets of some rough afternoons where Science High students found themselves in the company of Clinton High School if you know what I mean. Now a little further down the tracks, oh did I tell you I rode the subway to and from school, the number four train. As I was saying next to Science was the all-girls school Walton High School. Thinking about Walton brings a smile to my face. You see we got out earlier than they did. Many students jumped right on that train and started their trip home. But those of us who wanted some stimulation before we went home waited for the next train, the "late" train. That train brought us to Kingsbridge Road, the Walton stop, when the bulk of the girls got on. From that stop down to 161st Street it was, let's just say, an ongoing experiment is social education. Ask any Clinton or Walton graduate about the "late" train.

My mother often told me that I could be anything I wanted. My daily experience with teachers told me something else. When I didn't make the basketball team I was just there, directionless. So I spent my time playing ball and chasing girls and hanging out with my boys.

My grades in high school? Well let's say that As and Bs were a foreign language for me. I did eventually play on the senior basketball team while earning a 69 average for my three years at Clinton and received a general diploma. When I went to see the guidance counselor as I did in junior high school, he told me that I was not college material and should consider the military. There was no encouragement, no awareness demonstrated of other options. With no discussion of higher education and pathways to make up for my poor high school record, I left Clinton with no prospects, no direction and no encouragement, a sure path to the streets where all my friends were. They probably had the same counselor. There was a pattern of low expectation of success for Black kids which still exists far too often today.

My story could very well have ended right here had it not been for a girlfriend that I met during a track meet in Harlem at the 369th Armory. We developed a close relationship and one day in my apartment she asked me about the future and told me about a new school opening named Bronx Community College. She encouraged me to apply but since I had no experience with college I was hesitant. Undaunted, she got the application for me, sat me down at the dining room table and filled out the application. When asked what I wanted to major in I had no clue so we chose Electronics Engineering. With no expectations we sent off the application. To this day I don't know how or by what force or angel or maybe God was feeling generous that day but I was accepted to Bronx Community College. I big time ball player was a college student. "Now what" was the question of the hour. I had no clue.

Bronx Community College (BCC). They told me I had to register. Really? What did that mean? I walked into the auditorium amidst the din and was told to take a copy of the bulletin, take a seat and fill out your semester choices. That was the sum total of the process. I was totally confused. Since my application was for Electronics something, I found that page and registered for the courses it said I needed. 18 ½ credits. Seemed okay, a lot of science, some math, and history and gym. Okay, but what was lec., rec., or lab? They were listed for ever science course. That meant I had to have all three for each science course but no one told me that the three, lec, lab, rec were specific to each science course. S o I chose one from column a, one from column b and one from column c. This was my first disaster.

Add a dose of cutting classes to play cards in the cafeteria, a never ending pursuit of women, joining the wrestling team, playing with the basketball club and continuing to play ball at the neighborhood center, not only was it a disaster it was a disaster of nuclear proportions. At the end of my first semester I had a 0.38 GPA. My transcript had every letter in the book except the existence of that A for gym. There were Fs, Js for "over cutting" class, and Hs. I still don't know what the Hs were for. I had treated college like the rest of my life at that time. It was about having a good time with no commitments to my future or the troubles of the world and the plight of Black people both in America and around the world.

I had become a good wrestler and I would later be the captain of the wrestling team at Lehman College. It however looked like my college career was coming to a quick and unceremonial end. I often tell anyone who will listen that Bronx Community College saved my life. I had come about as close as I could to finding myself on the streets like so many of my friends. Randy went to prison as drug dealer. Winston became an alcoholic. Ray was shot to death at a party in the very neighborhood we had hung out a couple of weeks earlier. I saw Lena one day going to church. I hadn't seen her in a while. She was Mole's sister, my best friend. I excitedly walked up to her and asked her about Mole. What she told me would break my heart. She told me that they had found Mole's body floating in the East River. Mole was dead. I felt as if the wind had been knocked out of me. Yes Bronx Community saved my life. I was not expelled. I was to get a second chance.

I mentioned that I had become a good wrestler. Actually I was very good. I would frequently be the only BCC wrestler who won his match while everyone else on the team lost. Well with my grades I could just forget about wrestling. I had to sit and watch. I was in the stands when the heavy weights were ready to do their thing. That was my weight class. I stood 6'4" and weighed 226 lbs. The winner of these matches went onto the national championships in Minnesota. I sat there in the stands when the final match was to take place. One of the two opponents was someone I had faced. Not only did I face him, I had beaten him. Not only did I beat him I had pinned him in 38 seconds, 38 seconds! As he beat his opponent, he jumped up and down laughing and smiling as he received congratulations from his family and friends. As he basked I the glow of athletic bliss, I walked down the steps to the gym floor, went into the bathroom and cried like a baby.

I was off the team because of my grades. I also had to attend night school. I had to find a job. I spent some of the miserable times of my life working as a collection agent for the telephone company. I became focused on getting back to school fulltime, continuing my education and go were ever life would take me. I guess I also heard my mother telling me that I could do and be whatever I wanted to be. All I wanted was to get back on the team and become the national champion in my weight class. This goal, snapped me into reality. Because of the words and the impact of the guidance counselors, what I saw in my neighborhood every day, the memory of Emmet Till, my poor performance as a student and the growing movement for civil rights, I believed that I was intellectually inferior to the dominant group in America.

Perhaps my statement that BCC saved my life is on its face too dramatic but I don't think so. I did manage to repeat my courses and was readmitted to full time status. Ii did get back on the wrestling team, became the captain had the most wins of anyone else but fell short in my drive to be the national champ. BCC started a basketball team which I would lead as its captain and, after graduation from Lehman College, would be its assistant coach.

I entered college in 1963. You could say I knew something about the Civil Rights Movement seeping across the country and the assassination of John F. Kennedy. Closer at hand were issues around police brutality, racism and poverty. A new group named Simba had formed on our campus. They were founded by two Black students from Harlem. They stood for a corrected description of Black people and their history and addressing political forces that kept Black people in the back of the bus and in the specter of oppression and institutional inferiority. The name of the organization was taken from the struggle against colonialism represented by the Young Lions battle with Belgium over freedom. The Simbas were revolutionaries. With this as inspiration, the Black students expanded the global struggle for freedom to the all of Bronx Community College.

Their basic belief was that we were an ancient people with a history, values, spirituality and intelligence all of which was rendered nonexistent in order to justify the centuries old system of slavery, murder, rape and untold instances of dehumanization of and entire race of human beings. Blacks were written out of all history, occupied a position of subhuman beings and as had been previously stated had no rights. All elements of society upheld that criminal belief system. It was slavery and it was the law of the land. Any images of Black people were of servants or field hands. Simba believed that the real history of Black people in Africa, the United States and the Diaspora had to be told. I listened to them but didn't understand. I was living for the next party, the next girl, the next basketball team. After all I had watched the Tarzan movies. Wasn't hat the picture of Africa? My junior high school history books talked about slavery. It said that we were happy and showed a picture of Black people serving Mint Juleps to the master on the porch of the big house. Wasn't that what slavery was all about?

Simba believed that the culture of Africans was systematically destroyed in order to control those enslaved after being kidnapped from their homeland and transported to the west like so many bundles of straw or wood in the cargo hold on the slave ships. Simba also had a performing company that studied African culture through drumming and dancing, "The Simba Drummers and Dancers". I was encouraged to come and check it out. I did. I had no idea that my experience that night would change my life forever. Did I mention that I met my wife, the mother of my children, my soul mate at BCC?

The presentation that night was called *An African Journey Through Time and Space*. On the stage were four musicians with drums, one with a bell and one with flute. The lights were dimmed and after a brief introduction the drumming began. The power of the drums went right through me. It caused me to sit up and take notice. Then eight beautiful Black women dressed in African attire camo out on the stage and performed dances from West Africa. I was confused. The troop had pride, the drumming was inspirational but I was confused. This was not the stereotype of Black people who had no history prior to slavery. After all, a people with no history or culture had no future and could be enslaved, controlled.

I started attending Simba meetings, started going to the bookstore and became a voracious reader. My heroes became Frederick Douglas, Nat Turner, Harrier Tubman and Sojourner Truth. I was introduced to principles of human rights, freedom and liberation. I was presented the gift of Malcom X, his belief system and his evolution. I was also presented our loss when he was assassinated. According to Ossie Davis we lost our "Black Shining Prince".

Malcolm X and what he stood for, without question, were the most influential forces in in my life. I became a member of Simba, learned to play drums and African rhythms and became the President of Simba. The woman who would be my wife also became a member and a dancer. My life was to be a testimony to an end of oppression, and a victory for social justice. However I did not see my path leading to medicine and public health. I still carried the sense of inferiority in the deepest part of who I was. My activism included calling for an end to apartheid, demonstrations for African independence, demands for an end to racism and creating truth as it related to our people. Simultaneously organizations like the Black Panthers and their free clinics, the Young Lords and their free health care efforts and the Nation of Islam with their "You are What You Eat and Eat to Live" philosophy were gaining prominence. They year 1965 marked the creation of Medicaid and Medicare and the creation of the federally qualified health center (FQHC) movement. As important as these things have been proven to be, I did not see myself in that work.

I finished BCC. It took me four years to finish a two year curriculum but I did and went on to Lehman College which was the four year college connected to BCC. I continued to be devoted to athletics, earning letters in basketball and track and field. I was confident I had the intellectual capacity to major in Physical

Education. I remember being in awe of two Black women who were biology majors. I continued my activism with an on campus organization very much like Simba. One of our issues was our belief that all students majoring in Education had to study Black history as a part of their required course load. When we did not get what we wanted, we organized a campus wide lock in where we chained all the doors of all the building with the faculty and students still inside. We then held a massive demonstration. It was our original contribution to the campus building takeovers for a variety of protested demands. That include our support for the students who took Hamilton Hall on Columbia University's campus.

I graduated from Lehman with a B.A. in Physical Education and got a faculty position reporting coincidently with my first wrestling team who had always been a support. By the way, true to the man I had become, I boycotted graduation over racial and political issues. Years later I was honored as an outstanding alumnus and sat on the dais at graduation. Graduating forced me to see what I knew was the right thing for me to do. A friend and colleague helped me to see that I was underestimating my abilities to make a difference. He helped me to see I was still carrying the specter of inferiority that I had been carrying around all my life. At the same time, I realized that Physical Education was not going to be a vehicle to change the world, end oppression and enter an era of liberation and justice. I had a major breakthrough that filled me with clarity and strength. I needed to find a way to achieve my goals and vision. It came to me in the form of a new Master's Degree program in Black Studies at the State University of New York at Albany.

Armed with my new found self-confidence, and my long-standing commitment to change, I reached out to SUNY Albany. Yes, I did get accepted into the program and secured a position as a counselor for a program called EOP, the Educational Opportunity Program. This was a program designed to support students of color on their journey through undergrad. The Black Studies program was very rich, exposing me to more information, issues, political movements, African history and politics and gave me a sense of personal growth that would fill me with the skills and knowledge that I needed to make a difference.

I continued my involvement in and athletic life style and expanded into martial arts. My initial involvement came out an organized effort as a faculty member to break up drug trafficking at BCC. Of course when I found out about the Burundi Drummers and Dance I was ecstatic and became a member of the troupe.

I didn't realize how dramatically my life was to change how that would guide my steps for the next 45 years. There was a national movement in the Black community that called for a nation with in a nation. It said that we were a colony within the US. Those who were colonized had to be free and independent. It was The Congress of African American Peoples (CAP). I was an active member of

CAP and when I took a course called Problems in African Economies. The take home message was that no nation could be truly free and independent if it wasn't based in the sciences. The parallels were so clear to me. I would make the most significant difference by going into the sciences. The next obvious question was which science? What would be the most impactful? Which would make the biggest difference? Now that I had my confidence my mother's mantra, that I could be whatever I wanted to be, rang in my ears. If the people were sick and dying none of the other sciences mattered. My arrival at this revelation had taken many turns and within it, just beneath the surface, there more twists and turns to come.

Albany was good to me. I got married to my love of six years while in Albany. We had the most magnificent African wedding at an Akan temple. I became the first to graduate with the M.A. in Black Studies. I participated in the first National Black Political Convention in Gary, Indiana. But you never know what's around the corner.

After graduation we moved to Harlem. I got a position at Brooklyn College in another program called SEEK. It is similar to what I had done in Albany in the Educational Opportunity Program. My wife finished at Lehman College and worked at an alternative school on the lower east side of Manhattan. I taught a course in Black Revolution at The City College of New York and a history course in Long Island. The disappointment was my inability to find a full time position in Black Studies. You see I was trained as a generalist and the departments around the country wanted specialists. It was frustrating but you never know what awaits you around the corner.

Living in Harlem was special for many reasons. I became deeply involved with the cultural center of the Congress of African People, the House of Kuumba. Several of us who had been in Simba began new initiatives at the theater. We started an adult school offering the GED, a carpentry class, a political education program and a Transcendental Meditation class. I was at the center talking with my brothers and sisters when my wife who was pregnant with our first child called. I picked up the phone and heard those magic words "My water broke". I was a mess turning in circles, quickly announcing that it was time and, jumping to my car, I raced the mile and a half to the apartment to pick up my wife. I'm certain I was more nervous that she was as we sped down the East Side Drive to New York Hospital. This miracle of a new life about to be delivered was certainly one of the major influences that shaped my life. Ressie and I had made a decision to have a natural delivery. We went to classes to learn and prepare. We practiced breathing, focus and learned things to look out for. We were ready. When we got to the hospital, they took her to room where she would go through labor and then into the delivery room to have our child. I was given a set of scrubs, a mask and paper covers for my feet. Then things took the course that nature had designed. I was right there holding her hand, breathing together. But the delivery our child was to be done by a stranger to us, a Resident. We would work together and would soon see that crown of hair, hear that first cry and welcome our child into the world. My wife was a clinic patient and the resident who was about to deliver our child was a complete stranger to us. He had never seen my wife in the clinic. I didn't trust him but since I would be there at the delivery I would make sure that everything was good.

The pushing began. She pushed I pushed with her. The minutes turned into hours and the hours turned night into morning and despite the energy expended, our child was too big to make it through the canal. After a quick consultation, the resident decided to do a C-section. A C-section? That meant surgery and I was in shock. The team told me I could not go into the OR. There was nothing I could do. I had no trust in that resident or anyone else. At that moment all that I had learned about the abuses leveled against Black people, the racism, the oppression, Tuskegee, the horrors or slavery, the distrust felt in the Black community flooded into my mind. My family, my wife and my child, was in the hands of strangers and I did not trust them. No family should have to go through that. I had to do something. That moment brought a clarity that me would drive me to be an agent of change. The struggles against poverty, against racism and social injustice against inequity and access to life itself all crystalized my life's path.

One afternoon on the corner of 135th and Lenox Ave I was challenge by a member of the Nation of Islam about my life's choices. He told me that I wasn't doing enough. That my demonstrating, my Black Nationalism, my working with youth, my work with the Maisha Institute, my travel to West Africa on a roots discovery was not enough. To him I was playing a small game. He said at what we needed were doctors not drummers or artists or organizers. He said what we needed were doctors and that if I was serious about social justice, an end to oppression and to universal freedom, I needed to become a physician. I told him that was not my path I had no interest in a medical career. I said we needed Black folk in all the sciences as well as all the vital skills. He insisted and insisted. I was so forceful in my defense of me that the louder he became the more convinced I was that I was doing the right thing. I got on the subway knowing that I was right. Our pregnancy and impending delivery in the face of the absence of trust in white physicians and institutions made me rethink my position.

As they rolled my family away I was very concerned, saying to myself over and over again that no one should have to go through this. My community must be able to trust in those in whose hands we put their lives. Fate had given me direction. All my experiences up to that moment had placed me on that path. When clarity comes, connected to powerful images of the truth, one must accept that truth. What I had resisted became my future. I would surrender. The words, now spoken from my soul, I would become a physician.

Now that I had the confidence that my mother recognized decades before, it was not a question of how. It was not a question of overcoming obstacles. It was about getting it done. As a P.E. major I did not have the prerequisites for admission to any medical school. I worked one hour by subway to my job and one hour back. I went to the City University of New York in the evenings to get the courses I needed. I did this for a full year, including summer school. The results of this commitment to my vision was typified by my courses in Organic Chemistry and Physics, both of which I aced. I applied to 23 medical schools. I did well on the MCATs and was accepted to 11 medical school. I chose New Jersey Medical School because of the activist reputation of its Black community. True to form, I became President of the local Student National Medical Association chapter, then national president. True to form I was one of the leaders of the student-community occupation of a faculty council that was was going to expel four Black students two of which were seniors. I started medical school at the age of 29 with a two year old daughter and a fantastic wife. She finished Lehman and, in my second year, she was accepted to Rutgers Law School. I know it is controversial to give credit to Bill Cosby but, while much of America views the Huxtables as a fantasy, it was very real to us and several other Black lawyer and medical professional couples.

I have spent my entire life committed to freedom, social justice and equity. My decisions have always been made based on making the biggest difference. I chose Family Medicine over Orthopedics because Orthopedics was too distant from the people. I chose Public Health because of its community health foundation. I even found a way to serve during the over years as Director of the United Hospitals Adult Emergency Department. My career has included directorship of two health departments, one in Atlanta and one in Louisville Kentucky that was renamed the Department of Health and Wellness. I was on the board of the National Association of County and City Health Officials (NACCHO). I was the first chair of NACCHO's Health Equity and Social Justice Work group. My work has taken me to 14 countries in Africa, World Health Organization (WHO) special consultancies in Japan, Thailand and Uganda where we focused our attention on maternal mortality. I led a team, under the auspices of the Church of Christ, to Angola to address the issues of amputees and led a team to provide some mechanism to improve medical conditions in Goma, Zaire during the Rwanda genocide crisis. I started the first Center for Health Equity at a local health department in the country. My leadership skills and commitment elevated me to the top elected office of the American Public Health Association, its Presidency.

All of my experiences have evolved to the point that many say that I am seen as one of the national thought leaders in the Health Equity and the Social Determinants of Health movement. There is a growing movement that declares that health equity and the elimination of health inequity are social justice issues. My current position as Associate Dean for Health Equity and Community Engagement brings me back to the murder of Emmett Till and a shy boy in the Bronx who would eventually make a difference. My career and my life have been committed to raising the Black community out of the systemic racism and historical forces that continue to demonstrate community and individual health inequities. My career has been typified by a love of my people and a recognition that that you can bound over the obstacles placed in front of you fueled by the power of making a difference in a righteous cause.

This journey has not been taken in isolation. That baby born at New York Hospital has grown to become one of the leaders in art and revolution creating her own brand of magnificence and joy. We had a second child who has been moved by the continued presence of a commitment to bring about Social justice, Health Equity and a focus on the Social Determinants of Health. She has earned her DrPH and is making her own history. Their mother and I are no longer together and but I remain committed to justice.

My new wife and I have launched a new partnership in life and in business focused on creating solutions to health issues, locally, nationally and globally. She and her two children bring me full circle. The next turn surely will demonstrate my willingness to make life a fulfillment or our dreams.

CHAPTER EIGHT

Black Male Leadership

JOHN C. WILLIAMS, DRPH, MBA

"For Africa to me ... is more than a glamour fact. It is a historical truth. No man can know where he is going unless he knows exactly where he has been and exactly how he arrived at his present place."

—MAYA ANGELOU

It is my sincere hope that once you have read my story, you walk away with a sense of *who I am*, *where I've been*, and the *successes and failures* I've encountered along the way. I invite you to travel back in time with me – you're sure to have a good seat and a bird's eye view of my past, along with all the influencing elements yielding who I am today. As we journey along the way, it will be evident why I chose one path over another. Who knows, perhaps my story as it unfolds, might influence one or more of your own paths. Ready?

First, a brief reflection of my old neighborhood, and those responsible for planting the seeds for my life long journey – *a work in-progress*. My birthplace is in the state of Georgia; a small county whose current population is roughly 9,000, and a city one-third its size. To further put this into perspective, all residents of my town fall just short of filling the Atlanta Dome (Stadium) to capacity to watch a sporting event on a Sunday afternoon. Speaking of size, I am reminded of the town's kinship that existed during my childhood. During those days, walking to and from school – a two-mile walk, was routine and expected. You see, the town itself was a giant community whose sole responsibility was to contribute, however small, to the upbringing of every child in the neighborhood. This was done, primarily by the women of the neighborhoods, who proudly sat on their porch from early morning to late afternoon monitoring all community movements (vehicles and pedestrians). Walking from home to school (and back) each day had a certain calmness that built confidence and independence; both needed for character building.

I recall those of us walking to and from school were few in numbers. Like those before us, we needed guidance that could only come from the elders in the community. There were times when a gentle, but stern command to keep its precious cargo *on track* and in *place was needed* – today's equivalent neighborhood watch. Deviations from established pathways were met with a shout from one of its many Community Watchers, "*I see you and I'm going to tell your momma …*" Hearing this, I knew that a conversation with my grandmother, who raised me, awaited my arrival from school. This encounter, however gentle, was a mixture of raised voices and sleeked eyes, instilling the fear of God in my soul. The message was always the same – obey your parents or face brimstones in hell in "the here-and-after." After my grandmother had her say, hugs, kisses, and a gentle smile reinforced the deep-seated bond between grandmother and child, an inescapable phenomenon.

It is only now, as I reflect on my past, that the business of arriving to school, safely, and back home was a serious matter – as a child, I never gave thought to the contrary. I mean, why would I? After all, I was the child, and everyone loved me – so what was the problem? Of course, I had much to learn, and in time came to understand the unspoken and hidden rules, as well as the pitfalls of my town.

The Culture

The ethos of my town was the embodiment of two cultures, separate and unequal in many aspects. The balance of power, created by and reserved for the *power elite*, an inner circle of wealth bearers, comprised of the owners of production (inherited wealth), and those with high influence; club membership was exclusive. The common thread between the two forces, both owners and workers, was its innate dependence on each other for survival. The owners of capital needed a strong and willing labor workforce to harvest its crops; the labor force, strong and willing, provided the fuel needed to satisfy the needs of the owners. It was this combination that balanced this equation. While this working relationship between both parties had worked rather well during the days of the Cotton Gin, a slow but encroaching threat would add another variable to the equation, namely, *machine* – with this addition, change was inevitable.

My childhood, like other kids in the neighborhood, was filled with happiness, joy and a little sadness. The ladder set the stage for the roads I've traveled, crossing life's changing lanes, resulting in the man I've become. As I look back in time over my earlier years, I do so with a different set of lens. As a child, I only saw the present and what could be (future), a learned behavior driven by numerous factors, such as the inherent understanding of spoken words, facial expressions, body posturing, and other forms of communications by those with power over those without. Such powerful language served to keep the oppressed in darkness, only to be seen or heard from when summoned. In today's sophisticated world, such behaviors, rituals, and practices are recognized as cultural norms.

As I reflect on these good times, as they were, I am reminded of my community's unspoken culture, but well understood that existed at the time, and even to this day. You see, all kids in the community knew each other, as did their parents and parents before them. As kids reached their teen years, it was understood that cordial relations had to continue, as was necessary for the survival of all, but social ranking replaced childhood play, a firm and unbending rule. Depending on one's social status in the community, deviating from established norms, all but guaranteed violators unpleasant outcomes. The rules were put in place for a reason, and had to be learned, quickly and absolutely, for this was the law of the Land.

By age 12, I knew all the rules – there were many. The unspoken and/or spontaneous rules left little or no defense. You had only your faith and trust in God, your family's last name, and the honesty of your accuser. *Rules, both spoken and unspoken, had to be learned and continuously cultivated; there was no substitute for a good education, for it, and only it ensured an opportunity for success later in life.* The premise behind this belief was that once knowledge had been acquired (technical or theoretical), it could not be taken away, ever!

As I grew older, more freedom of expression (verbal and physical) was allowed by my grandparents – I roamed beyond the boundaries of my very small world, which spanned two blocks in any direction from my domicile. A silent, but powerful voice provided clear and safe passage from one section of the city to the other. Childhood conditioning (norms, work ethics, bible studies, etc.) were matched with a combination of good hearted and caring neighbors for its youth. The threat of my saying or doing this seemingly new freedom gave rise to frequent trips (jogging), literally, from school to home for lunch – often times there was no lunch to be had, and I knew it – this, simply, was an exercise in futility, aka, male pride. Even so, giving the impression to classmates that a table spread of delicious awaited me was the order of the day. Those trips, in time, would serve to etch who I would become. *For now, I only knew that my destination, however far away, was linked to education – for this was the only sure way to success.*

Economic Plight

During the late fifties, and before then, farm land was culled and cultivated by man and animal. Typically, laborer and animal (mule) were connected by a series of ropes and a simple ply (farm instrument), needed for turning the soil for seed planting afterwards. The process was day long, starting and ending from the rising of the sun to sunset, respectively. Throughout the day, the only hint of communication between man and animal are the commands of the worker, given to the animal, and a trained response (behavior) from the animal to comply. In other field settings, laborers were in high demand and sought after by farmers to work the fields and perform any other number of chores, including gathering tobacco, picking cotton, and unearthing potatoes, to name a few. These were by any measure, good times for all, both owners and workers. The system in place, had worked for generations. No thought for change in method or process was ever considered, though the system was grossly inefficient. Owner's profit margin from their crops had made each a millionaire many times over, largely off the backs of the laborers. The workers' work ethics and established affinities with the owners provided a conduit for virtually free labor – still, a better choice for the workers than its alternative.

Despite the good times, it was enviable that old and established systems would give way to new models of operations. Technology (Age of Agriculture), the new frontier challenged the old ways, and its handlers. The new tools, tractors, favored the owners of production and lessen the demands for the once sought after and needed field worker. Overnight, the number of workforce workers had been reduced by half. The coming of Ages guaranteed no return to the past – the skills learned, nurtured, and practiced from earlier times were replaced with emerging technology. Those (workers) capable of mastering the new breed of technology were assimilated; those without the skills, knowledge, and abilities to adapt found themselves without work and unable to care of their families.

Economically, the loss of jobs forced close-knitted families and friends to seek opportunities in other parts of the country, a condition that further divided a people already divided – technology knows no faces. The toll taken on families, good or bad, was immeasurable. The lesson learned was clear – *getting an education and/or unique set of skills had to be at the forefront of the few, the proud, and the faithful.*

Another memory which stands out was the town's annual carnival – it was nothing short of magic. This was an event that all would turn out to see and take their place as either participants or onlookers from afar; even farmers, who only came into town once a week for restocking of feed for their animals and grocery shopping for their families. For this special occasion, all would put on their Sunday's finest to bear witness to this yearly event. Other special days, such as the Fourth of July, Christmas, and Labor Day were also celebrated, but were treated as any other ordinary day of the year. The economy during those times showed neither respect nor favor for special days or events. Bills still had to be paid, and mouths fed, and children clothed. Birthdays! One's birthday was always special to him or herself, but often not celebrated, unless it occurred during the school year. As for myself, my first birthday party occurred at age 25, when my wife invited me to dinner where I was joyfully greeted by family members and friends. That day ranks as one of joys in my life.

God's Gift ...

Grandparents

My grandparents raised me, along with six of their own children from birth. Why was I raised by my grandparents? Unfortunately, my mom passed away while giving birth to me. Her unexpected death set into motion uneasy tensions between the two families; both families wanted to raise my sister and me under the same roof. A series of discussions and debates over which family would raise the two of us pursued, resulting in no amicable solution. The matter was resolved through the legal system. It proclaimed that my sister was to be raided by with my dad (Pennsylvania), and I would stay (Georgia) with my grandparents.

In retrospect, the decision to split and raise us in different environments created an unintended injustice that can never be made right. Despite best intentions for visitation throughout the years and to spend time with each other, economics and hard times took its toll on our childhood relationship, resulting in feelings of emptiness, sadness, and homeliness; I've carried this uneasiness within me all of my life. Today, my sister and I have a wonderful and close relationship, though we have worked at it! In retrospect, was the right decision made? I think not. Nevertheless, I am blessed to have been raised by my grandparents. It is only now that I understand my unwillingness to lay anchor in any one place too long – a childhood issue, for sure. *The lessons learned from my childhood experience are the cascading ills bestowed on the innocents, despite its good intentions.*

My grandparents were natives of Georgia. Both were very passionate towards others – often times and throughout my childhood, I recall their giving no thought to taken in the children of others, treating and caring for them as their own children. Their passionate for others was not limited only children, but as well to strangers (adults) passing through the town, looking for work, and with no place to call home. Little thought, seemingly, was given to inviting unfamiliar faces to the kitchen table and offering them a place to sleep for the night. There were times when some lived with us, as a family member, for several months before packing and moving on. Of the children, whose brief sprint with us, and adults passing through, my siblings and I knew only as cousins and uncles, respectively. It was not before my reaching adulthood that I knew differently.

My grandmother was very religious woman. Her beliefs in religion ran deep; she lived by and practiced her faith and taught her children the same. As a member in the household, the Sabbath was always respected and adhered to. It seemed that learning the Bible and following its teaching was in parallel, often exceeding, that of formal schooling. Ironically, both were important and necessary for survival and character building. The frequency of church attendance, from childhood to adulthood, was inspiring. I have often given thought to becoming a Baptist minister – this thought, lies in the shadows of my dreams.

For a brief period of time, my grandmother was an elementary school teacher. She had only a 3rd grade level of education. During the time of her teaching, a high school diploma was not a requirement at the time of her teaching. While I don't remember her teaching, I do remember her job as housemaid. Her duties in this role including caring for the children of others, cooking, cleaning, washing and general house duties. There were times when her day was extended to accommodate guests of her employers for some type of evening affair. Upon arriving back to home, after these occasions, she would mutter words, very softly as though she was talking to herself. Not fully hearing or understanding her words, it was evident that a better future for her children was on her mind. Both she and my grandfather were very careful and selective in their conversations with us about the plight of our environment and that which resided within. This, of course, was done an as effort to ensure our planned and safe escape from our plight to a better place, a clear message if there ever was one – *a good education for a better life.*

My grandfather, a *sharecropper*, was a hard worker, never taking off time to rest, except for the Sabbath. His work day began with daily call of the yard rooster, about 6 AM, and often ended with the fading of the Sun. Educationally, he had only a 2nd grade level of (formal) education. Beyond his limited education, there were no requisites to be a sharecropper – some of the desires included having a protestant work ethic, trustworthiness, a Christian, and to be family man. Ironically, he had something else, which he called *"mother-wit."* This was, according to him and others of his time, a gift from God. In my youth, I had heard that some people were blessed with special talents and skills. Now, this was something, I thought to myself. My own grandfather had been blessed by God almighty himself – *must be good*. After bombarding him with questions, for which he had no answers, he simply looked at me, gently smiled, and said that he did not fully understand this gift, but that God had given him everything he needed to make a living and take care of his family —hearing that, I was satisfied — I sought not to press the issue any further, for in time, I would come to understand more about this special gift.

My grandfather had responsibility for all field hiring, and paying field workers for their day's work. As the years past, I began noticing mistakes in overpayment to field workers he would sometime make, resulting in less payment for his work. Bearing witness to this, I assumed the role of assisting him with paying the workers – he was happy and relieved. I saw this as my opportunity to take responsibility for something I enjoyed doing, that is, working with numbers. As I reflect on this and other endeavors, I note that my grandfather, though not educated, was indeed a very bright man. God had blessed him with an abundance of people skills – he had the respect of all in his company, plantation owners, field workers, and friends. I spent most of my childhood modeling his every move, it seemed. It was most important to me that I learn as much and as quickly as I could, for I feared our time together was destined to be short lived. *The road to success was deepening.*

Learning Curve

As I alluded to earlier, I was born in Jim Crow South, a tiny town approximately 200 miles south of Atlanta, Georgia. My elementary school was a one-room house for first graders; kindergarten followed a few years later. I was always quite inquisitive about my environment, including all its properties residing within. By the time I reached High School, my interest in science and math had reached boiling levels. All of my free time was spent on reading books of science and attempting to solve algebraic problems. Like many young adults, I was all but certain what awaited me in the near future, but was certain my trajectory would deposit me in either science (medicine) or math (engineering) – I was confident that I had the will and capacity to be successful in any endeavor I chose to follow.

As life would have it, in the shadow of my dreams to become more than I could imagined in life was the stalking of the Selective Service. All young men, by law, were required to register for the Draft. I had no issue with draft registration, and knew if called that I would opt for Officers Candidate School (OCS) – seemed simply enough. This path, if came to fruition, would serve to support my much sought after education. There was no immediate threat; I had at least a year before receiving notification for draft induction.

This was a system where your name was placed into a lottery pool for future draft induction. The process was, in theory, quite simple – those with low lottery numbers stood to be selected and drafted ahead of those with higher lottery numbers. During those times (late 60s and early 70s), I began noticing the frequency young men I knew (*classmates from the community*) who had all received low lottery draft numbers. All others had received high lottery numbers. Could this be happenstance? I put my limited knowledge about probability to work. I sought verification of my findings and assumptions from college statisticians.

Shortly after the end of the draft lottery, researchers wrote and published books about the fairness of the draft lottery system. It was most interesting to me how a town with so young men of color had all received low lottery numbers. Further, it seemed, very low lottery numbers for non-white young men of that same community, whose population was significantly higher, received much higher lotter numbers. This is not to say that others did not serve in the military, I'm sure they did; however, those that did serve seemed to have done so in non-combative areas and/or were in placed in positions of leadership where fighting on the front line posed minimum risk of bodily injury. Finally, if members of the higher population of the community received low lottery numbers, I know not of any returning to the community, from Vietnam, in a body bag.

At age 18, I registered for the draft, a requirement for young men, during the 60s. This was the era of the Viet Nam war, a controversial war. All eligible persons fit for duty were issued a *lottery* number by Selective Services; depending on the lottery wheel, one was subject to be drafted and sent off to war. The process of selection was simple, but questionable – the lower your lottery number, the higher the probability of being drafted. Well, wouldn't you know it! My lottery number was 005! By now, I was all but certain that more than probability was at stake – *and it was.*

In the late 60s, I received my draft card with a Classification of 1A with an accompanying lotter number of 005, a combination that all but guaranteed a trip to Vietnam to fight for unknown cause and undeclared war. At the time of my induction notice, I was living in New York City, and was a full time student. I requested and was granted a hearing to appeal before the Local Board of Selective Services to plea my case for an extension in order to complete my training. My Board denied my request, and I immediately appealed their decision. I wrote my Local Board a letter, questioning their fairness or lack of, and sent copies of my letter to upper-level military personnel requesting their intervention on the grounds previously stated. After a few weeks of waiting for a response, my case was put on hold, pending further investigation. A few months later, my request for an extension was granted, with the implicit understanding that another lottery drawing awaited me upon graduation. This was the beginning of many encounters I had with my Local Board. Interestingly, Local Boards of Selective Services consisted of members of the community (e.g., farmers, merchants, doctors, and others of influence). Members of this esteem club were the same people that I had known since childhood. Their decisions were never challenged. Why would anyone challenge an *unbiased lottery pool*? Most certainly, not members of the labor force, for they had been trained all of their lives not to question orders, mandates, or requests – all missing variables that blocked balancing the equation of fairness.

City of Brotherhood

During my teen years in Georgia, I often spent the summer months with my family in Philadelphia, PA. Those summer visits allowed for family bonding on my dad's side of the family; it also relieved my body of endless hours of hard field work in Georgia's blazing sun. As mentioned elsewhere in this chapter, my mom's family was spiritual and god-fearing. My dad's family it took religion to another level. My uncle and pastor of the church conducted Noon day prayers, daily, Monday thru Saturday. Sunday's worship followed – a day's event, giving thanks to the Lord for life, health, and strength. Attendance, though not required, was expected of all, and all attended. This ritual has been in place my entire life, and continues to this day. The point of this is intrinsic character building that can only be learned through spiritual engagement.

I often asked the church elders, "why so much praying"? The response was always the same. That is, "We pray for our young, the innocent, and unknowing. We pray that you, in time, will learn to be thankful for what you have, to be humble, protect those who can't protect themselves, and have the wisdom to do the right thing and make the right choices." In time, I came to learn, understand, and appreciate the meaning of those spoken words, especially *wisdom*. As I *reflect* on those spoken words, I know truth lies on one side of the equation and challenge on the other. Even now, I am guided by the voices of my past elders, for it keeps me on my guided path. Those teachings, from my elders, and others like it have helped to shape the man I've become with all the dressings and ribbons my elders hoped and prayed for.

In 1969, I was admitted to the School of Radiology Technology, a two-year hospital based program, located in New York City, NY. The cost of training was $450.00 for two years, which I did not have. I borrowed the money from my uncle, who had attended and completed the program earlier. The $450 dollar tuition feed to attend school was paid back to each student, as stipend over 18 months at $25 per month. Upon completion of training, a nationally board exam was administered. Passing this exam was a sure guarantee that all field work was behind me – *clearly, this was a success by all measures.*

Prior to graduating from radiology school, I was drafted and called to serve my country. Having spent two years of my life training to work in the healthcare field,

I had already set my mind on applying to medical school. After a series of letter writing and phone conversations with the draft board, I was granted a deferment.

Big Apple

After leaving Georgia, I moved to Pennsylvania. My plan, educationally, was to apply to either Temple University or The University of Pennsylvania. Before applying to either, I received a phone call from my uncle, who lived in New York City. He called to let me know that an opening was available to attend school for training in radiologic science and technology and asked if I would be interested in applying for admission. I applied for admission, and was accepted into the program as a full time student. At the end of the summer, I relocated from Philadelphia and moved to New York City, two weeks before the start of the school. Shortly after arriving in New York, I asked my uncle for an explanation for the available seat. The reason was simple – the available slot, previously held for his younger brother, had been drafted into the military and ordered to report to his nearest draft station.

The training program, radiology science, only accepted eight students per year; it was a two year hospital-based program. The curriculum was a mixture of didactic and on-the-job training (a.k.a, apprenticeship). It was also fully accredited by all the accrediting bodies, including the Joint Commission for Hospital Accreditation (JCAHO). I thought it a gift from God and wondered why me! The answer is three-folded: First, for the first time in my entire life, I was in a professional setting, inside of a building with air-conditioning, seeing and feeling the radiant heat of the Sun only when I decided it so – I wondered if *heaven* was as nice – funny, huh! I would often pray that I not be awaken from what was surely a dream. You see, back in Georgia, during my childhood, I had worked the fields (picking both cotton and tobacco during summer months, digging up embedded potatoes from the earth (winter months) and a host of other field work tasks doing the year. There were times when my siblings and I worked the fields well past the start of school, which typically started in August, as I recall. Most kids lived on the farm and were needed to help their families harvest field crops. Often times, the needs of the family and economic conditions delayed the start of their ability to attend by 2 to 6 weeks – such conditions, seemingly, were understood by both classroom teachers and school principal – *this was the life of the few.*

Second, six months into the training program, a stipend of $25 dollars per month was issued to each student. To this day, I still remember receiving my first check – not knowing any better, I asked my uncle, who had recruited me, if the money was really belonged me, which he acknowledged in the affirmative. Twenty-five dollars – this was the first time in my life that someone had given me money, and not wanting to take it back, to I mean by over charging for purchased items. The the cost of the two-program attend was $450.00 – the $25 monthly check was given back as a stipend. Though the hospital received free labor, the students received technical skills in a field (healthcare) with very high demands for those learned skills. From an investment perspective, the return on investment was significantly higher than the cost ($450) over two years.

Third, my purpose in attending this specialized training was to learn all the program had to offer, and there was much to learn. By the second year into the program, I had become fully adept in the techniques of radiography, and was able to match any senior level radiographer in its application. Additionally, I fully understood the science that ensured near-perfect imagery (bodily part of interest) after exposure to radiation. Human anatomy and physiology, topographic anatomy, and radiation physics had become second nature. I had only planned on practicing radiology for a couple years, and then go to medical or engineering school.

At the end of the training program, all students were required to sit for a nationally recognized examination, administered by the American Registry of Radiology Technology (ARRT). Upon passing this examination, a designation of R.T. (Registered Technologist) would was placed behind one's name. Lettering qualified those who passed the examination to work in any state in the country. Prior to graduation, all graduates of the program had received several offers of employment. My specifically, I was offered employment at the facility, Hospital for Joint Diseases & Medical Center. A year later, I was offered the position of Assistant School Director at New York Medical Center and Flowers & 5th Avenue Hospitals. My role was to assist in creating a new School of Radiology, a two-year hospital based program, and serve as technical supervisor of staff.

During my tenure at the New York College-Flowers and 5th Avenue Hospitals, I sought to continue my education. I had an opportunity to attend New York Medical College esteem medical school. Unfortunately, I lacked the guidance needed and failed to take advantage of the opportunity. I opted to attend another program, one that offered those with two-year Certificates in Radiology Sciences. I applied for admission and was accepted into Manhattan College, School of Engineering. The program offered three tracks under the broad umbrella of Radiological and Health Sciences. These tracks were health physics, management, and education. I completed the program within two years and was awarded a Bachelor of Science degree – though not my dream degree, it served its intended purpose. By now, I was married and had a family – medical education was put on hold; family obligations took precedence. Shortly after graduation, I moved my family to Atlanta, GA to care my ailing grandfather, the man who had raised me from childhood, and given so much of himself to ensure my success in life.

Peach Tree State

In 1977, my family and I relocated to Georgia, a place I had not known since leaving in 1968 years. Pondering the move to Atlanta, I had made it my business to keep abreast of its local politics. My wife and I researched all there was to know about this new place we would call home and raise our beautiful two children. Having secured employment prior to relocation, I saw no need to question all that I had researched. Finally, we were in a place where the school system was good for our children, we lived in a middle class neighborhood, the environment was clean, and the need to fight New York City traffic was a thing of the past. Further, I was to connect the dots of getting from where I was to where I wanted to be. After all, what could possibly go wrong with this plan?

Perhaps, most exciting about living in the City of Atlanta was the flamboyance of its young debonair mayor, Andrew Jackson. Shortly after moving to Atlanta, I met the mayor Jackson at Grady Memorial Hospital. He was there because his son had hurt himself and needed radiology services. I introduced myself, told him that my family and I were newcomers to the city. He welcomed me and gave me an overview of the city, including some of its local politics. As leader of this expanding city, he had done his job – his interpersonal skills were impressive and true to form, a true sign of a leader. During the late 70s, Atlanta was coined a boom town; job prospects were high, cost of living was low, and the city's population exploding, especially among professionals and entrepreneurs. Geographically, the city favored both national and international travel, especially by plane.

At the time of relocation, my son was three years of age, and my daughter, an infant, both born in New York. My wife, a native of New York City knew nothing about southern living, but wanted to spend her life, as least part of it, visiting and living in different cities, and countries abroad. Her grandparents, who had raised her, were from the Virgin Islands. Neither of them had stepped beyond the perimeter of New York City since arriving some 40+ years earlier.

By the late 70s, Atlanta experienced an economic downturn, a sharp contrast from five or six years earlier. I remember the intentional efforts of the Phoenix police department to recruit police officers from the Atlanta. Mayor Jackson was upset, and told his officers that Phoenix had nothing to offer them. His efforts to keep his force were not successful; salaries offered by Phoenix were much higher than that of Atlanta.

My wife, highly educated and the holder of a college degree from Ivy League New York University, sought to secure a position in the Fulton Elementary School System as a classroom teacher in special education – she was not hired, though there were positions available. After weeks of searching for a position in her field, and not finding one, she applied for a job at McDonald's restaurant, where she worked for a few months.

Lone Star State

In 1979, shortly after my grandfather had passed away, I took my family to Houston, Texas. First impression was not favorable, due in part to being robbed within hours of arrival. It was very large and open city; it looked very western and *lawless*. Upon arrival to the city, we stopped for the night, about 3AM, and checked into a hotel located not far from the world renowned Texas Medical Center. Feeling nervous about our unknown environment, I left the room and walked outside to check on our personal belongings, locked and left inside our U-Haul trailer. I walked to the rear of the U-Haul trailer, noticed the broken lock, pulled open the closed doors, and saw only emptiness. Further, the license plate bolted to the trailer was missing as well. In the late 70s, you might recall the gas shortage (late 70s), the days of *odds* and *even* license plate numbers. For example, a license plate number with an even number, say 20 meant one could purchase fuel on a Monday; alternatively, odd plate numbers meant purchase on a Tuesday.

Before going back to the room and telling my wife what had happened, I first went to the front office of the hotel and informed the desk clerk of the robbery. At my request, she called law enforcement. A police officer arrived on site, wrote and gave me a copy of the incident report, apologized for the incident, and suggested leaving the area I found myself. My wife and I contemplated returning to Atlanta, but knew that was not a viable option. We reasoned why we had left Atlanta in the first place, a sagging economy.

Since we were in Houston, we decided to stay for a few days to explore employment opportunities. All indicators pointed to an abundance of jobs for technical and professional workers. During our first week in Houston, the same week of being robbed, I walked the streets of the Texas Medical Center in search of employment. Virtually, every building had wanted signs posted in its windows seeking workers of kinds. I came upon and entered a hospital that advertised for a Department Head of Ancillary Services. I applied for and was offered the position within 48 hours of my interview. We had placed our troubles in God's hand and swore to travel the path laid out for us – this was *blind faith*.

Having no place to live or call our own, we lived in a hotel for the first few weeks. Afterwards, I rented an apartment, where we stayed for the first two years, and then purchased a house – all was going well. I worked at this facility for several years before accepting employment at one of Humana's three hospitals in the Houston area. The hospital I transferred to was about 40 miles east of Houston. Demographically, it was about 90 percent Caucasians and 10 percent Black. During my first week on the job, I took note of the delivery of supplies, chemical fluids needed for film development. A person of color, known by all staffers, delivered those products to the department on a weekly basis. Without these special chemicals, film processing was not possible. A few hours after the delivery man had vacated the site, same day, a distasteful comment was made about him. Ironically, the comment was made by a hospital professional of high status. Shocked by the comment, I pondered how long this ridicule had gone on, and considered that day as being my last day at that facility. The next day, I spoke with the person of interest, expressing discontent over the earlier remark. I was told that the comment was in poor taste and would not happen again. Later during the week, I shared my conversation with hospital administration. They, too, apologized for the comment, and then acknowledged that the culture was in of need change; further, it would take time to change old habits, and that I would be an agent of change – I wasn't sure how to interpret what they had said. I was well aware, by virtue of the town's proximity to Louisville, that the population of the minority was low, I didn't know how low. In all fairness to the community, race relations posed no threat to the community; there was no need to discuss what did not exist. As years passed along, I had become a fixture in the community, policemen officers, local officials, and citizens knew who I was, where I worked, and the company I worked for – I posed no threat to anyone or the community.

Now, I thought to myself, would be a good time to get back on track with my dream job, though I recognized that medical school was nearing the boundary of my radar. My son and daughter, 7 and 4, respectively, had taught me to balance my time. Medical education was again placed on the back burner, in exchange for graduate degree in business (MBA) – academically challenging, but straight forward. By now, experience had taught me that academic excellence was the only real option, short of luck, open to me. Following the conferring of my graduate degree, I hungered for more education; this time, I sought a second graduate degree in public health. This degree, coupled with a business degree would unlock all doors of opportunities – that was my thought. Bearing witness to the many doors I saw opened and/or closed forced a truth I wanted not to believe, even though I had been taught, from childhood, to see the world as though it was water, for it was always changing and would be shaped by others capable of doing so.

Educationally, I have always modeled a path for my children to follow. Was I wrong? The answer is no, I was not wrong for instilling education and the need for achieving as much of it as possible. Simply put, one cannot have too much education, I reasoned. Further, education allows one to build, if s/he so desire, their own doors! There are those with high levels of education (*e.g., physicians, lawyers, engineers, etc.*) whose keys (education) have not and will not open certain closed doors – a harsh reality of life.

Valley of the Sun

In 1989, I was recruited to Phoenix City, Arizona to work in one of Humana's six flagship hospitals, Humana Hospital-Phoenix. My reasons for accepting the promotion was based on a combination of my innate need pride and discontent. First *pride*, my previous hospital in Texas had undergone an inspection, conducted by the Joint Commission. The hospital had received full accreditation. There was no better or greater accomplishment – my department, in particular, had done exceedingly well on all counts for the first time. I recall having received phone calls from hospital administrators inquiring what questions had been asked of me by the Joint Commission surveyors, and how I had answered the same; further, they asked if I would avail myself to assist in the preparation of their own upcoming inspections. I felt honored to have been asked and offered my assistance. On the question *discontent*, I did not feel appreciated by my then current employer. Several months later, I was presented with an opportunity transfer to one of Humana's flagship hospital. After my interview with administration and staff, I was offered the promotion, and accepted it.

Upon arrival to Phoenix, Arizona, I noticed the modernization of buildings and clean streets, a noticeable difference from Houston. The air quality posed a threat as untimely dust storms formed and shaded the area brown. Surprisingly, Phoenix had a high prevalence of asthma among its growing population. I discovered that the high rate of asthma was due, in part, to the transportation of plants, small trees, and flowers brought to the area by those who had relocated from their place of origins. Demographically, Phoenix's population was approximately 1.2 million; Blacks or African American accounted for 4 percent.

I was given responsibility to manage Medical Imaging, a department far larger in size and staff than the one I had left. The issues and concerns awaited my arrival proved to be complex and challenging, both of which I welcomed. I knew I had the skills, knowledge, and abilities to navigate in rough waters. Of interest, Phoenix was a city of a diverse community (e.g., race, ethnicity, etc.); ironically, leadership of this fine institution chose to follow *a behavioral style of management*. Workers falling under this umbrella of management (masses) assumed their learned roles – *seeing this was reminiscent of earlier times.*

As I recall, the chief radiologist and I had lunch together on my first day on the job. A few months into the job, the assistant administrator, who had recruited me, informed me that he had been offered and had accepted a promotion at another Humana Hospital. He then congratulated me on my action plan to address the issues for which I was recruited. My staff, a mixed audience, had grown accustomed to their own independence, going and coming as they pleased, doing and/or refusing to respond to managerial requests. I began meeting with them in an effort to pinpoint their concerns and issues, whether personal and otherwise; I gave each one space to vent their anger and hear their plea, and as for me, I sought to gain their trust and confidence, for I knew that a change in culture was needed, but unsure how long such a change would take, given the climate that of the environment. How does one change the culture in an environment where promises had been broken, past practices had become the norm, institutional tenure for top leadership short-lived, departmental management was spotty, at best, and was void of management theories and techniques. These issues, coupled with the interventions of hospital administration, rightfully or not, throughout the years, had served to be the source of its downfall. Unfortunately, their involvement was driven and necessary for their own survival – promotions rested on the successful achievements of the departments for which they were responsible – this was an example of top down management.

Relocating the family to Phoenix was not part of the initial plan – the idea was for resolve departmental issues, and then return to Houston for completion of my studies. We gave thought to changing our initial plan, and considered relocating the family. We all loved the landscape (e.g., mountains, valley, and four seasons), and the educational school system was cutting. By the time we were ready to make the move, my son, then an 11th grader received an invitation to attend the Naval Academy – all bets were off. We decided to wait until after he had finished high school. We tried again, this time, my daughter, now in the tenth grade, gave reasons to stay put, to which we honored. Having exhausted all options but one, I moved back to Houston, re-enrolled in the School of Public Health, University of Texas-Health Science Center, and continue working on a master's in public health. Nearing completion of all coursework, I began looking for employment. There were few jobs and lots of competition for the few advertised; the Texas Medical Center was a magnet for the entire country, it seemed. I completed all required coursework for the master's, but had not written my theses. Rather than write a theses, I began taking advanced courses and decided to petition for doctorate status in public health. A recruiter called me and asked if I would be interested in discussing a high level position in Louisville, Kentucky. I told him give me a couple of days to discuss the matter with my wife, and that I would call him after doing so. The only thing I knew about Kentucky was that Toyota had a plant there – long story short – I was offered and accepted a hospital management position in Louisville, Kentucky.

Bluegrass State

1995, I was recruited to Louisville, Kentucky to manage the Department of Medical Imaging (Diagnostic, Ultrasonography, Nuclear Medicine, Specials, Vascular, CT scan, MRI, Bone Densitometry, etc.) My scope of responsibility spanned throughout the city, as well as Southern Indiana. The department was vastly larger than the one I had managed in Phoenix, Arizona. Its level of sophistication included cutting-edge technology, renowned researchers (from across the country, and some, from other countries); the famous Heart & Lung Institute; and the Hand Transplant Center, first ever performed in this country. In 2010, Jefferson County, Kentucky's population was roughly 741,000 thousands, with Whites representing 74 percent, Blacks or African Americans, 21 percent, and others, 5 percent.

With respect to my employer, company branding began the first day on the job, and became a *constant* that resided in the equation, always to be referenced in business and casual conversations. Orientation for newly hired high-profiled professionals was a class act, not to be copied nor imitated by competing interests – it had all the makings and trimmings of a perfect relationship that needed daily feedings to calm one's ego – not necessarily yours. Additionally, doors really were opened for you, though acts of kindness and respect, on the part of those with lesser positions. In general, the campus, externally and internally was very clean, so much so that it looked out of place, once off campus. Upon entering unfamiliar buildings, patients and visitors were greeted, and assistance to reach their intended destinations (e.g., physician appointments, parking garage elevators, etc.).

After leaving my previous employer, I sought employment with county government. I was most interested in applying knowledge and skills, previous learned years earlier. I submitted an application for employment to the Kentucky Department for Public Health; a short time later, I was notified of an opened position, County Public Health Director/Health Officer, to manage the affairs and operations of two adjacent county health departments. I contacted the agency and expressed my interest in the position, and was interviewed, and offered the position. Educationally, I was well equipped and prepared for the daily operations of the job. To my surprise, at the time of my hiring, I was the only County Public Health Director in the Commonwealth of Kentucky, possessing public health education; as well, only a few directors were holders of a master's degree. I say surprise because my experience had taught me that more (education and experience) was the norm. I found this to be intriguing and sought to find answers – this process took not long at all, for the answer was simply and understanding on a number of fronts. First, persons in these positions, primarily in rural areas had had these positions ranging from 15 to 30 years, long before the master's degrees and/or public health education showed up under the radar screen. Second, and perhaps most importantly, directors of public health agencies, traditionally, were members of their own community, both a credit and potential deficit to the community, depending on the pleasure of board members, responsible for oversight. As best I could gather (Intel), virtually one-hundred percent of all county administrators were either born or raised in the county of which s/he managed, or was from an adjacent county – in short, everyone knew each other.

Public health, by definition, is political. It is, mostly, invisible until some catastrophic event occurs (e.g., 911, SARS, smallpox). It permeates the community at all levels (e.g., city, county, state, national, and international). Though, tasked with educating and communicating with the public, this phenomena is a both positive and negative, as was evident during recent events of the past, which left local communities out of the loop, with respect to communication. We are all aware of the adage, public health is a local matter – this tends to be true, especially at the local level.

My years in this position were well served, as I was able to apply knowledge learned, skills gained, and abilities achieved in addressing community health issues and concerns in both counties served. Also, it provided me the opportunity to meet with and discuss public health issues with state, county, and city officials. During my tenure in this position, the Association of Health Directors (AHD) met on a monthly basis to new and ongoing issues and concerns of the day. At times, invitations to attend our meetings were extended to state legislator(s); this served to maintain established relationships, engage officials of policy issues, and request support for advocacy of composite issues during legislative sessions. Under my leadership, both county agencies achieved growth not experienced before my time. Of significance, all outdated computers were replaced with state of the art computers, making for first time usage of internet capabilities; electronic banking, direct deposits – the last two mentioned caused a scare, as staff had always gotten handled their pay checks, physically – all now routine.

After working in this setting for seven years, and having accustomed to addressing many issues that were similar in nature and solution, I began exploring process analysis – I attempted to flowchart procedures for understanding, and then automate the same for training – a simple idea with the ultimate aim to standardize procedures and increase effectiveness. Additionally, I explored other issues of substance that warranted deeper analysis – this practice, though innocent at heart, did not go unnoticed. From this point and forward, I was certain, even after seven years, that I was an outsider – environmental culture was at stake.

In 2009, the University of Kentucky, College of Public Health (CPH) recruited for a position to work at the college as assistant professor (non-tenured track). My wife and discussed the pros and cons, and I agreed to leave my employer. I reasoned that it was a good move, and would place me in an environment of like peers with common interest. In 2012, still an employee of UK, a former student (Associate Professor) from China, who had taken a policy course from me, earlier, sent me an invitation to teach a summer course in policy and politics. His government was especially interested in learning about the Patient Protection and Affordable Care Act (PPACA). Towards the end of my stay in his province, I was asked as I would go to three other provinces and teach the same course – time constraints only allowed my visits with two of the remainder three. Upon returning from China in 2012, I took a position as assistant professor (tenure track) with the College of Health Sciences, Department of Clinical Sciences. Environmentally, I'm afforded the space and flexibility needed for the body of work of which I'm engaged. The campus, a composite of academia and practice, is a draw for many of our students, as well as faculty and staff. Culturally, the workforce is comprised of several ethnic groups, each of which is significantly smaller than the primary group.

Synopsis

What now? Where am I? Am I where I want to be? Has it been a worthwhile ride, all these years? Were the dice fair? Did my expectations of life overshoot the realities of it? Hmmm – is it better up there? Life's rotating Merry-Go-Ride, seemingly, slowing down for some as they climb abroad, speeding up as others attempting the same – did they make it? If so, who are they? Where are they now? Of education, wasn't this the key that would allow passage to the Magic Kingdom? What about all that training and experience, collected from childhood to now? Though useful and needed, and sometimes lifesaving, *kinda*, can't it be marketed? And, what about mankind – you know, those onlookers from our past, and the futurists, observing as we fade away in timeless space. See it as you may, but the usefulness of sharing and imparting of one's knowledge, skills, and abilities, is little more than collective memories of a short stay on planet earth!

My journey, thus far, has been one filled with both joy and pain, exceeding both limits. Nevertheless, *moving forward* is and has always been the order of the day. Hibernation, while good for some species of animals, is not so good for man – think about it – one school of thought suggest an abundance of jobs, waiting in the wings, following a sharp downturn in the economy; for others, open enrollment in closed quarters, if not engaged in the labor force, irrespective of the economy – *ironic, isn't it?* This isn't good or bad – *it simply is.* The funny thing about one's experience is the reality of it, and depending on the particulars, it can be either harsh or less so, resulting in changed behaviors. For some, life is good, rewarding, and sometimes boring. For others, life can be both good and rewarding, but is often challenging, unrewarding, and not fully appreciated. It is apparent, whether spoken or not, that lives are different and can only be viewed and understood from the perspective of the target of interest – this is so important. Personal wealth, for some, gives a pseudo, but real sense of power, unmatched by the lesser, whose eyes are forever looking upwards into the Heavens and whispering, "How long, how long, and He answering back, Not long, not long."

Several months ago, I was asked if I would take part in contributing to this book. I believed myself quite lucky to have been asked. As I began writing, I quickly came to the conclusion that this writing was unlike that of previous research and editorial papers I frequently write – this was very different and personal, due in part to my having to delve into my childhood, long buried, hurtful and sad experiences of my life, and calling forth all that has contributed to making me who I am today. Indeed, we are all shaped by our past. Until the writing of this chapter, I had always avoided that which needed not be avoided. Even with all that I have written, there lies beneath my Teflon, but penetrable shielding, that part of me that begs for exposure, but is too hurt to surface.

Happiness in life trumps all, even when our every expectation falls short of the goal post; happiness, no matter the amount, is a blessing and should be treated as such – *God hears and sees all?* On the issue of conformity, a powerful variable of control, capable of forced compliance with established environmental and organizational norms – economics, the need for individual inclusion, and one's propensity to succeed ensures adherence to the rules; club acceptance for a shot to the top, is a function of many factors, some written (*procedures*), others non-written (*social norms*).

Lastly, what does it take to successfully navigate in today's society and world? The short answer is God's blessings. With this, depending on other factors, not clearly identified, must be a very strong and unbinding work ethics; a willingness to navigate in unchartered waters; a drive to achieve the highest level of education, both in theory and practice; a deliberate desire and commitment, in spite of barriers placed in your path, to succeed. None of this is easy, but is expected. The road to success is easy for some, and harder for others. The old adage, "You can do anything you set your mind to do" has credence to it. Not every child will grow up and become the leader of the Free World, the Pope, or any number of other notable titles – this is okay. We should aspire to do what we believe we would be best at doing. I imagined myself wanted to study medicine and law. I did neither – life changes the rules, sometimes, in midstream. We make adjustments and move forward – *such is Life*.

We live in a global society, separated only by the boundaries of geography. Modern transportation has given rise to increased competition for a shrinking workforce, not only in this country, but abroad as well. If you are contemplating your future, what to do, where to start, and how, my suggestion is that you prepare for tomorrow by first doing a few very simple things today, such as removing from your vocabulary words and phrases that have negative connotations, e.g., can't, maybe, blame, etc., and replace the same with, I have the will and capacity to succeed in my efforts – doing otherwise only serves to impede one's progress in life; well defined goals and objectives must be the center piece of a career plan. As stated elsewhere, life has been good to me. Certainly, I have had my failures, but I'm all the better because I learned from my mistakes.

At the end of each day, I always end with a prayer, giving thanks to Him for allowing my family and myself a safe return to our homes. I pray for a better world, better relationships between and among the different races. We talk of increased diversity, but have little to show for it. Finally, I pray for mankind, asking for forgiveness for all us, our sins and ill behaviors, and good will to all.

CHAPTER NINE

Some Concluding Thoughts

MAUREEN P. BEZOLD, PhD, MPH AND STERLING J. SADDLER, PhD

"Never underestimate the power of dreams and the influence of the human spirit. We are all the same in this notion: The potential for greatness lives within each of us."
—WILMA RUDOLPH

In her 1977 speech at the Nobel Banquet, prizewinner Rosalyn Yalow addressed the students of Stockholm, identifying them as "the carriers of our hopes for the survival of the world and our dreams for its future." Yalow spoke of an ever-widening circle of learning. She said, "If we are to have faith that mankind will survive and thrive on the face of the earth, we must believe that each succeeding generation will be wiser than its progenitors. We transmit to you, the next generation, the total sum of our knowledge. Yours is the responsibility to use it, to add to it, and transmit it to your children."

You have read about leadership and organization culture and climate. You have also read about seven extraordinary men who have succeeded despite the odds. If you read closely, you may have noticed several themes mentioned in a number of the chapters. Many of the leaders whose stories you read mentioned role models. Others point out how important mentors were to their success. Several of the authors also talked about how important it is to be familiar with an organization's culture. This knowledge or the lack thereof can make or break your ability to successfully lead an organization. You may also have noticed that social activism, service to one's community and faith also influenced our leader. Finally, you may have concluded that most of our leaders are servant leaders whether or not they identified themselves that way. We close with a straightforward brief discussion of role models, mentors and organization culture that captures the value of role models, mentors and knowledge of organization culture to leadership success.

Role models can make the most profound of influences on what we do or do not do with our lives. While we typically think of role models as positive that might not always be the case. I'm sure we have all been either appalled or chuckled when we've heard a tiny little child say something naughty not knowing that what they said was naughty in the first place. Why did he or she do this? Because of role models. So be very careful in whom you choose as your role models. Be sure that your role models reflect who you want to be both as a person and as a professional. While we think of role models providing examples of what to do in both our personal life and career there are people who can serve as role models of what not to do. We can think of people that have done things that we say to ourselves "I'm NEVER going to do things the way John Doe did them". Be sure to keep those lessons in mind too. As you consider who would make a good role models think of the men in this book. Their careers, their accomplishments are inspiring. We consider them role models and you might want to follow suit.

The Value Mentoring Brings to Success

Mentors are critical in our growth as leaders. Our mentors guide us with the wisdom they have acquired over the years and, ideally, they will keep us from making mistakes they have either made themselves or they have witnessed others make. A mentor is someone who has experience with the challenges that trainees face, the ability to communicate that experience, and the willingness to do so. A mentor takes a special interest in helping another person develop into a successful professional.

The role of a mentor is different from that of a supervisor or adviser, although these formal academic roles can lead to a mentoring relationship. The essence of mentoring has been described in a report by the National Academy of Sciences as being an adviser, teacher, role model, and friend (National Academy of Science (NAS), 1997). We would add one more component to that mix: advocate.

A mentor might be a faculty adviser, a laboratory director, a fellow student, another faculty member, a wise friend, or simply another person with experience. Mentoring relationships are critical to launching successful careers and, at a minimum, necessary to adequate career development within the field. Typically, a mentor is an experienced advisor and supporter who guides and trains a junior colleague (Underhill, 2006). Mentors help mentees to learn basic skills of their career practice. They also communicate formal and informal rules that guide ethical decision-making (Levin, 2005).

References

From Les Prix Nobel. Rosalyn Yalow—Banquet Speech at the Nobel Banquet, December 10, 1977. The Official Web Site of the Nobel Foundation. © 2003 The Nobel Foundation. Accessed July 10, 2003. Retrieved from http://www.nobel.se/medicine/laureates/1977/yalow-speech.html.

Levin, L. C. (2005). Lawyers in cyberspace: The impact of legal listservs on the professional development and ethical decision making of lawyers. *Arizona Law Journal, 37*, 589–624.

National Academy of Science (NAS). (1997). *Advisor, teacher, role model, friend: On being a mentor to students in science and engineering*. Washington, D.C.: National Academy Press. Retrieved from http://stills.nap.edu/html/mentor/.

Underhill, C. M. (2006). The effectiveness of mentoring programs in corporate settings: A meta-analytical review of the literature. *Journal of Vocational Behavior, 68*, 292–307.

About the Editors

Maureen P. Bezold, PhD, MPH, is Associate Professor of Health Sciences and Social Work at Western Illinois University. She received her doctorate in strategic management at Virginia Tech and her MPH at the University of Wisconsin–La Crosse. Dr. Bezold has worked in public health emergency preparedness with both large urban and small rural health departments. Her research interests include public health workforce management and capacity building in public health organizations. She is also interested in how forgiveness education can reduce violence and emotional labor in organizations and how it can improve personal health.

Sterling J. Saddler, PhD, full Professor of Educational Leadership, is former Dean of the College of Education and Human Services at Western Illinois University. He served as Professor and Vice President of the Office for Diversity and Inclusion at the University of Nevada, Las Vegas (UNLV) and was Founder and Executive Director of the Center for Workforce Development and Occupational Research. He also served as interim Associate Dean of the College of Education at UNLV and Chair of the Educational Leadership Department. Prior to joining the UNLV faculty in 1998, Dr. Saddler served as Dean of Academic Affairs at the Center City Business Institute in Syracuse, NY. He is well-published in the areas of workforce education and development with an emphasis in leadership, curriculum and dropouts, and has secured millions of grant dollars through local, state, regional and federal agencies.

About the Contributors

The individuals featured in this book were chosen because of their personal experiences while climbing the leadership ladder in their respective fields. These are individuals whom we felt were not afraid to tell their true stories as African American males within their respective organizations. They each possess the authentic transparency necessary to tell their stories without fear, and the stories they tell capture lived experiences, as opposed to what the leadership volumes tend to say about what "should be"; they have come up through a system less open to inclusiveness, and are not afraid to describe these experiences candidly. Their experiences, beginning in childhood with family and community life, have shaped the men they have become.

***

Janice L. Glasper, MEd, RDMS, RVT has served as the Director of Health Programs Advising and Limited Entry Admissions at the College of Southern Nevada (CSN) for the past three years. She began her professional career in Radiologic Technology after receiving an Associate of Science degree from the University of Nevada, Las Vegas (UNLV) in Radiologic Technology, followed by a Bachelor of Science degree from UNLV with emphasis on Ultrasound Technology. In 2004, Ms. Glasper earned a Master of Education in Educational Leadership/Workforce Education, also from UNLV. She has held various leadership positions in her years as an imaging professional as well as during her tenure at CSN. In addition to having served in various roles as an imaging professional in the Las Vegas community, Ms. Glasper has served as the Coordinator of Sonography Clinical Education, Director of the Sonography Program, Department Chairman, and Director of Achieving the Dream.

Alphonso Simpson, Jr., PhD, is a native of Andalusia, Alabama, and full Professor and Department Chair of Liberal Arts and Studies at Western Illinois University. The department offers programs in African American Studies, Religious Studies, and Women's Studies, and Dr. Simpson' work is in African American Studies. He is also a board member on the National Council for Black Studies, where he currently serves on numerous committees. In Chapter Two, Dr. Simpson brings us knowledge, experiences, and perspectives using the lens of black culture, including family, community, and spirituality. He relates this to the lived experience of a black man working in higher education.

Georges C. Benjamin, MD, is a well-known health leader, practitioner, and administrator. He is Executive Director of the American Public Health Association (APHA), the largest public health professional association in the U.S., representing public health professionals and academics around the world. Dr. Benjamin works extensively at the federal level to affect health policy, and was the first African American to serve as Secretary of Health for the state of Maryland, the top governmental health professional in the state. Dr. Benjamin has also been identified as one of the top black health professionals in the U.S. In Chapter Three, Dr. Benjamin shares his unique personal experiences while climbing the leadership ladder. His belief that being in charge and being in leadership are separate ideas is a message he communicates throughout his chapter.

John R. Lumpkin MD, MPH, FACEP, FACME, FAAN is Senior Vice President at the Robert Wood Johnson Foundation, the largest philanthropic organization in the United States dedicated solely to improving the health of Americans. He previously served as Director of the Illinois Department of Public Health, the highest governmental public health professional in the state of Illinois. He served as an activist in the Civil Rights Movement, and this interest in activism was piqued by his parents' extensive efforts in labor union and community organizing, to improve life in both the workplace and the community. In Chapter Four, Dr. Lumpkin brings us the perspectives of social justice and fairness that have guided his career choices. Throughout his career, he has combined these perspectives with his medical education to offer better health outcomes to the communities in which he has worked.

Sherwood Thompson, EdD, is Professor and Assistant Dean, and former Chief Diversity Officer, in the College of Education at Eastern Kentucky

University. Dr. Thompson has directed campus-wide diversity and inclusive excellence programs at five universities and conducted research in diversity and social justice for over 25 years. He has also served as President of the Association for the Advancement of Education Research. Although Dr. Thompson focuses on improving the well-being of individuals, he brings a slightly different perspective than the other contributors. Dr. Thompson works in multiculturalism and internationalism, serving as Director of the Office of Third World Affairs at one point in his career. In that position, he worked to educate the general campus community about issues of concern to international and multicultural members on campus, as well as in the broader community. In Chapter Five, he explains that sometimes those whom you believe to be your advocates as you seek to effect positive change fear potential repercussions and prefer the status quo. Dr. Thompson has learned over the years that listening rather than talking is critical to being an effective leader.

Dr. Keith B. Wilson, PhD, MEd, is Professor at the Rehabilitation Institute at Southern Illinois University Carbondale (SIUC). He has previously been Dean of SIUC's College of Education and Human Services, and served for 15 years as an administrator and faculty member at the Pennsylvania State University. His research interests include cross-cultural/multicultural issues among persons with disabilities and privilege based on phenotype (e.g. skin color and gender) in the United States. Dr. Wilson has been honored with several service and research awards, including the 2012 Researcher of the Year Award from the National Council of Rehabilitation Education; the 2013 Virgie Winston-Smith Lifetime Achievement Award, presented by the National Association of Multicultural Rehabilitation Concerns; and the 2014 James F. Garrett Distinguished Career in Rehabilitation Research Award, presented by the American Rehabilitation Counseling Association. He was recently invited to participate in the Healthy People 2020 Law and Health Policy project as member of the Report Working Group for Disability and Health, of the Centers for Disease Control Foundation, in collaboration with the U.S. Department of Health and Human Services (HHS), Office of Disease Prevention and Health Promotion (ODPHP), and the Robert Wood Johnson Foundation. In Chapter Six, Dr. Wilson shares his personal experiences, opportunities, successes, and obstacles in the academy.

Adewale Troutman, MD, MPH, CPH, is Professor, Associate Dean for Health Equity and Community Engagement, and Director, Public Health Leadership and Practice, at the University of South Florida in Tampa. In addition, he is former President of the American Public Health Association. Dr. Troutman has successfully assisted in getting one of the strongest anti-smoking regulations in the country passed and implemented. He served on four national advisory committees for the Secretary of Health and Human Services involving Infant Mortality Reduction, Healthy People 2020, and two Institute of Medicine reports. In Chapter Seven, Dr. Troutman will provides his insights about leadership and addresses the question, "How did I get here?" He tells his personal story about growing up "po" in an urban environment to becoming a well-known and respected professional in the public health world.

John C. Williams, DrPh, MBA, was Assistant Professor (retired) in the Department of Clinical Sciences at the University of Kentucky, and had a long career as a healthcare professional. He has served in various capacities at the American Public Health Association, including as a member of the Intersectional Council Steering Committee and Chair of the Health Administration Section. Dr. Williams has also served on the Association of Schools of Public Health DrPH Concept Identification and Specification Task Force. In 2012, Dr. Williams was invited by the Centers for Disease Control and Prevention to serve as a program evaluation consultant for the Division of HIV/AIDS Prevention. In Chapter Eight, he describes the trials and tribulations associated with growing up in the deep South, and highlights the value of taking opportunities when they present themselves throughout your career. He continues to seek professional advice from others, such as family, church and community members, and professionals in leadership positions.

ROCHELLE BROCK & CYNTHIA DILLARD
Executive Editors

Black Studies and Critical Thinking is an interdisciplinary series which examines the intellectual traditions of and cultural contributions made by people of African descent throughout the world. Whether it is in literature, art, music, science, or academics, these contributions are vast and far-reaching. As we work to stretch the boundaries of knowledge and understanding of issues critical to the Black experience, this series offers a unique opportunity to study the social, economic, and political forces that have shaped the historic experience of Black America, and that continue to determine our future. Black Studies and Critical Thinking is positioned at the forefront of research on the Black experience, and is the source for dynamic, innovative, and creative exploration of the most vital issues facing African Americans. The series invites contributions from all disciplines but is specially suited for cultural studies, anthropology, history, sociology, literature, art, and music.

Subjects of interest include (but are not limited to):

- EDUCATION
- SOCIOLOGY
- HISTORY
- MEDIA/COMMUNICATION
- RELIGION/THEOLOGY
- WOMEN'S STUDIES
- POLICY STUDIES
- ADVERTISING
- AFRICAN AMERICAN STUDIES
- POLITICAL SCIENCE
- LGBT STUDIES

For additional information about this series or for the submission of manuscripts, please contact Dr. Brock (University of North Carolina at Greensboro) at r_brock@uncg.edu or Dr. Dillard (University of Georgia) at cdillard@uga.com.

To order other books in this series, please contact our Customer Service Department:

(800) 770-LANG (within the U.S.)
(212) 647-7706 (outside the U.S.)
(212) 647-7707 FAX

Or browse online by series at www.peterlang.com.

www.ingramcontent.com/pod-product-compliance
Ingram Content Group UK Ltd.
Pitfield, Milton Keynes, MK11 3LW, UK
UKHW022239230426
12048UKWH00018BA/1362